What people are saying about

The Fallen Women of Mythology

This is a deep dive into understanding how misogyny is woven into the fabric of our society so deeply that women perpetuate it upon themselves. Outlining cultural misogyny on every level of society, this book shows the systematic disempowering of women who deserve recognition, and erasing women that gain notoriety. This is an eye-opening book, and brings into focus the archetype of the fallen woman and how shame was used to subjugate the power to create life.

Lady Belladonna LaVeau, Archpriestess of the Aquarian Tabernacle Church

Lady Haight-Ashton's well researched comprehensive treatise on *The Fallen Women of Mythology: Goddesses, Saints and Sinners* explores the "divisional line between the ancient matriarchal and patriarchal way of thinking" about women and their place in society. This literary work of redemption reveals unique and compelling details, lost and hidden for centuries, about women purposely mis-portrayed by patriarchal historians as domineering, aggressive, sexually immoral, and/or in some way deviating from the cultural norms of their eras. As Lady unveils a litany of the lives of legendary women, many of whom are well known in religious myth and lore, she takes us on an emotional roller coaster ride. For readers interested in Female Spirituality and Herstory, this inspiring book is a gem.

Rev. Gypsy Ravish, Singer/Writer, Clan Mother Alexandrian Witchcraft Kent Line

Pagan Portals

The Fallen Women of Mythology

Goddesses, Saints and Sinners

Pagan Portals

The Fallen Women of Mythology

Goddesses, Saints and Sinners

Lady Haight-Ashton

MOON
BOOKS

London, UK
Washington, DC, USA

CollectiveInk

First published by Moon Books, 2024
Moon Books is an imprint of Collective Ink Ltd.,
Unit 11, Shepperton House, 89 Shepperton Road, London, N1 3DF
office@collectiveinkbooks.com
www.collectiveinkbooks.com
www.moon-books.net

For distributor details and how to order please visit the 'Ordering' section on our website.

ISBN: 978 1 80341 636 6
978 1 80341 641 0 (ebook)
Library of Congress Control Number: 2023943983

Design: Lapiz Digital Services

UK: Printed and bound by CPI Group (UK) Ltd, Croydon, CR0 4YY
Printed in North America by CPI GPS partners

We operate a distinctive and ethical publishing philosophy in
all areas of our business, from our global network of authors to
production and worldwide distribution.

CONTENTS

I would like to thank my husband Iain Haight-Ashton for his continuous support and to my three Manx cats who never leave me alone for a single minute, sitting beside me as I write. They want to be part of whatever I do! And thank you to the Goddesses of old who have allowed me to channel into the past to discover the stories in this book.

Foreword

I am again excited about the story of women that Lady Haight-Ashton has brought to those who carry this work forward into the centuries to come. She has brought forth names of women and Goddesses whose stories have been in the shadows far too long. Ask yourself how any more are there? In my experience the Magick and power these women possess have importance in our world today. Through this writing I myself am much more aware of the progress women have made in leading us to the forefront where we belong once more.

Laurie Cabot

Preface

I am a Priestess who writes about women with a dancer's spirit and soul. The ancient stories in this book are like unfulfilled dances that need to be revived. It has been inspiring to uncover the mysterious lives of these wayward women, many whose stories have been hidden or lost.

A few years ago, I choreographed a dance entitled *Veils*. I believe this dance offers a unique parallel that characterizes my broad definition into the fate of fallen women. It is a classical dance for four women. With the sounds of drumming in the distance upon a stage filled with fragrant incense, three dancers move in a slow procession onto the stage. They are completely hidden under one large black diaphanous veil. I am the fourth dancer who walks behind and is separated from the other dancers. I too am draped, except with three veils instead of one like the other dancers.

As the drumming quiets and music begins to come through the sound system, the three dancers suddenly pull away the veil that has covered them with a sweeping motion to reveal their figures. Still veiled, I stand facing the audience completely motionless. In turn each dancer sashays around me with balletic steps and carefully pulls away one of my veils. Not using the veils to re-cover their faces or figures, instead they spin and twirl the delicate captured fabric above their heads in joyous freedom. Finally, I am left standing veilless. Slowly awakening, I begin to dance with passionate pirouettes, circling the stage with abandon, before we four dancers suddenly run off the stage in quick processional movements. I believe this dance mimics the domain of the *Fallen Women of Mythology*. These shrouded dancers are like women who entered the world veiled within the context of ancient mores until they abandoned the restraints of restrictive society. Though sovereignty is momentarily intoxicating for these dancers, they still feel compelled to run off the stage disappearing from the audience as if secreted away.

I have been a ballet and modern dancer who now regularly performs Sacred Ritual Dance. Early religious cultures had created a thin line between what is acceptable or not. Ancient Priestesses who performed sacred temple dances in the context of religious ritual were highly respected. But those who performed in public beyond the confines of ritual were described as belonging to the class of fallen or sinful women.

The figure of the fallen woman has been widely portrayed through literature, art, and dance for thousands of years. Moving on to the last few centuries we have the works of Dante Gabriel Rossetti the 19th century English poet, illustrator, and painter. Another artist of the period was George Frederic Watts, who was a British painter and sculptor. Both were associated with the Symbolist movement which focused on dreams, imagination, and spirituality. These artists among many others helped to define a woman's role amidst 19th century societal restrictions. Their works captivated a wide audience and helped to propel the fallen women's enduring myth.

Within the context of this book, I will explore the hidden pages of history to uncover herstory and the true value, of these ancient fallen women. I will look beyond their so-called sins and misfortunes in the re-telling of these remarkable stories for all to appreciate.

Blessings,
Lady Haight-Ashton
Priestess of the Goddesses Lilith, Selket, Hecate and Isis

Introduction

I like to compare ancient stories about fallen women to leaves on a tree. Eventually the leaves tire of dangling and detach from their branches. Fluttering in the wind as they reach their destination, they land softly upon the ground. Sometimes they are disfigured and land in great piles of fellow leaves only to be sweep up and discarded. Other times the leaves fall in pristine condition to be admired by a passerby as a treasured seasonal souvenir.

Whether Goddesses, saints or sinners, similar storylines of fallen women were tossed together in one mass of misunderstood myths destined to be disregarded, gathering the dust of antiquity. Yet as with leaves that fall safely to the ground, many stories of fallen women over the centuries have survived only to be immortalized and admired in fantastical art and literature evolving into almost mythical souvenirs of a forgotten time.

How can we understand history without acknowledging herstory? Which facts are real and which have been fabricated in the abundance of varied tales about the fallen women of the ancient world? Myths often began as collections of folkloric and moral stories that defined the belief and culture of a civilization. Handed down through the centuries by word of mouth or printed in ancient texts, many of these tales evolved into more fiction than reality, crossing the boundaries into mythology. Saints started as sinners and Goddesses morphed into saints. Stories developed a life of their own, following the ethical values of the period with a misguided judgement often the outcome. Myths have their origins in truth.

How does one define a fallen woman's persona. The most acknowledged characterization is that she has fallen from the grace of God, because she was morally unacceptable in her deviation from the social and cultural norms of the era. Written history and verbal hearsay tell us she was guilty of many roles that cannot be easily defined. She was a prostitute or perhaps a sexually manipulative warrior Queen, or simply an undervalued woman who was accused of acting out any number of behaviors that constituted socially improper or offensive acts. She was castigated for being too independent, knowledgeable, unconventional, or undeniably mystifying. Behavior as defined by the culture and the age forced these women to exist in a mist, seen but not seen. Have women been so judged historically because the worship of the Goddess within the concept of the Divine Feminine had been replaced with one male God across many religious beliefs thousands of years ago? Here began the plight of woman's untrue character.

For thousands of years the term fallen woman has expanded vastly beyond one's perception of an unchaste woman. In referencing famous historical sinners such as Eve and Mary Magdalene to the arcane and foreboding Goddesses of ancient mythological lore such as Hecate and Kali, the word fallen becomes an umbrella term that fits within a wide range of errant settings all monitored and condemned by the court of male hierarchy. As in the judgment of Eve in the Garden of Eden, her bite of the forbidden apple and subsequent explosion caused a ripple effect that is still felt today within too many female populations. However, Adam bit that apple also. He joined Eve in her expulsion, yet biblically and historically he does not endure the burden, that sinful Eve was forced to carry for all womankind.

Within the many possibilities that could constitute a characterization of a fallen woman, she really becomes a contradiction and enigma within herself. In the broad world of historical art and literature her many likenesses have been portrayed as romantically attractive or tragically alluring figures. History has thus created a kind of mythological conundrum around her image.

Whether thousands or just hundreds of years in the past, we have the many wayward Biblical women and the female sinners of Christendom so often portrayed in art and literature as sharing many of the same temperament and characteristics. But we also have a group of women who have not seen much notoriety, those branded as the painted ladies of the night. They were the hidden yet flamboyant Goddess like Courtesans of history, who succeeded in their profession by breaking all the rules of traditional society. Though certainly thought of as fallen women they became in many cases successful and very independent entrepreneurs. All women who chose to travel the different roads of prostitution, were defined as fallen whether they floated in and out of the profession as family necessity dictated or made it a full-time career.

Was it a distorted vision inside the thoughts of the primordial patriarchal establishment that feared the female archetype whether Goddess, saint, or sinner? Perhaps too often the fallen woman image was the result of bewilderment within the male consciousness who did not fully comprehend the female principle. I interpret her semblance as more of a victim than the enemy. Her dilemma is one of false impressions and maybe just a disparity of common opinion. The fall from grace becomes the heavy yoke that mythology and history tell us she must bear. I see it not as a yoke but a release from the preconceived notions of what the ruling hierarchy of the ancient world constituted as appropriate conduct. The fallen women of mythology were rebels who knew their own minds, and who valued their sovereignty. They should be embraced not spurned.

The divisional line between the ancient matriarchal and patriarchal way of thinking is best described by this analogy: being dutiful and subservient brings safety and acceptance while craving recognition and independence whether wild or tame, carries the burden of the fallen feminine persona.

Throughout history matrimony was often considered a safe haven for women, or was it? Thus, any unwed woman was out in the open, prey for false accusations and condemnation. Her virtue was oftentimes on trial until she was securely placed in the confines of male protection within marriage. Sadly, the loss of virtue for an unwed woman meant she would face dire consequences imposed upon her by the so-called principled courts of the age.

Tracing back our history to around 25,000 BCE, archeologists have found clear evidence that our prehistoric ancestors valued women very differently because they understood and revered the Divine Feminine, as the supreme creator. As humanity evolved and the old order of hierarchy changed there was an evolution away from the Goddess and mysteries of the feminine. Yet some cultures were able to hold onto their belief and still worship the Goddess in the open. Others were forced into a clandestine practice of great secrecy. The power of the feminine began to collapse along with the shift in the identity of what distinguished a good woman.

There are now three main world religions: Christianity, Judaism, and Islam. Many of the ancient creation myths beyond these three male dominated faiths did incorporate a Mother and Father creator ideology in one form or another. For example, one of the Egyptian cosmologies tells how the world rose from the waters of the Nu, infinite and lifeless, through the darkness of chaos. What emerges from the waters is the pyramid shaped mound called "benben" which ultimately gave rise to the sun God, Ra. Another aspect of the Egyptian myth is that the world rose from the primordial cosmic egg, perhaps an analogy for the amniotic fluid within the womb and a strong feminine image. Water as the dawn of life and the feminine elemental becomes a prevalent theme in many early creation myths.

It was the controlling new dogma of the Christian view that violently sweep the ancient world, causing societies to suddenly shift theologies in favor of a more universally male dominated hierarchy. Then with the advent of this new way of patriarchal thinking, adding the perpetual fear of the unknown along with the steadfast influence of the matriarchal, cultures were turned upside down. No longer was the Mother Goddess the sole creator. The masculine God as the Father suddenly took over as the creator of all. The Goddess as Mother fell from her previous importance only to survive in a lesser role as subservient to the male God, taking with her the valued status of women for over a millennium.

We know that the Christian belief incorporates a Father, Son, and Holy Spirit. Thoroughly patriarchal, the Christian belief is vague, which raises questions as to the interpretation of the Holy Spirit. The Holy Spirit is generally defined as the third person in the Trinity and thought to be the Triune Godhead manifested as three in one. In many religious orders the Holy Spirit is seen as the feminine amalgam in the Goddess Sophia, the feminine side of God.

The ancient Judaic sects continued to acknowledge a male God as they had for thousands of years with women relegated to a submissive role. One example is that of the ancient Israelites who restricted women's behavior greatly. The permission of a father or husband was needed for an unmarried or married women to leave her home for any reason. Women were thought to be separate from men, thus they also had to pray separately. Within many ancient Judaic groups, the opinion of the rabbinical scholars had been that women were vein and feared because they were the cause of men's uncontrollable lust. Moving forward, the view of the modern Jewish woman is a bit perplexing to say the least, with the perception of women going against the ancient beliefs and conventions. Depending upon the sect whether Orthodox, Conservative, or Reformed, some women are still shrouded behind wigs and hats while most are free to lead their lives as they choose, many becoming powerful and influential leaders.

Islamic women even to this day are not really considered equal to men. Sadly, in the purest sects, women are still secreted away with head and body coverings such as the hijab, burka or the more extreme covering of the niqab. With the morality squads in Iran and similar authorities in other muslin states, women are still hidden and concealed away from one's vision. And any thought of a woman falling away from the accepted norm, whether her fault or not, could result in death by stoning or beheading.

Through the ages similar judgements and punishments including the burning of thousands of so-called female Witches during the 15th to 18th centuries came down upon sinful women by God, Yahweh. and Allah. I do not want to expound upon the histories of these religious tribes, except regarding their thoughts on the feminine. The definition of a fallen women is the same whether Chistian, Jewish or Islam and it is these combined religions who also hold the responsibility for the subordination of the great Goddess.

Many women of independence and substance, leaders and trailblazers either became sinners of some sort or deleted from historical texts where they were downgraded to the category of fallen. But in many circumstances, referring to Christendom, when an act defined as sinful was committed, repentance sometimes brought forgiveness and sainthood as with the purported sinner Mary Magdalene. Much has been written about Mary Magdalene because she is so potent in our historical and spiritual teachings. Women from every culture and ethnicity can feel a bond with her memory. Once labeled fallen, her popularity within all beliefs caused her to suddenly become pardoned from her alleged sins. Thus, Mary's story becomes a prime example of sainthood bestowed, as a consequence of patriarchal discipline. With the power of her enduring influence as a threat why not cleanse away her sins and proclaim her a penitent saint? Her true identity as a teacher and possibly the wife of Jesus conveniently washed away within ancient text.

Like Magdalene, there is an even more fearsome fallen woman, perhaps the original in ancient biblical text. In Isaiah 34:14 she is referred to as the screech owl. She is a nocturnal creature and her name is Lilith. She is always with us. She was the first partner of Adam and to many one of the first Goddess symbols. She fell quickly and was never reprieved. Images and stories of like-minded fallen women permeate the millenniums mythologies.

Let us also consider the many women of mythology who have not sinned or became penitent saints, but who have merely become lost because they have disappeared between the cracks of the common early historical and theological texts. Their value badly underrated or simply ignored. Now slowly some of these early records are being discovered anew and being reevaluated.

The historian Herodotus, born around 484 BCE in Halicarnassus, an ancient Greek city now located in Bodrum, Turkey, wrote about women as mostly having secondary roles in society. The accuracy of his histories is widely debated now, but at the time they served to educate the populace. In contrast he not only writes about women in minor roles, but as leaders and sought-after oracles. Here we have the confusing, and differing stories of the lost women of Herodotus, unfairly missing from the annals of ancient archeological findings.

The Nabateans were a very ancient tribe of nomadic peoples from north-western Arabia. Historians calculate that they probably settled in the region of Petra, now an ancient archeological site in Southern Jordan as early as 7000 BCE. The Nabateans worshipped the Goddess Al-Uzza, along with her triad sisters Al-Lat and Mena, thus becoming the Goddess of the Morning Star, the Mother Goddess and the Crone Goddess of fate and time. Archaeologists have only recently acknowledged evidence of a temple at Petra honoring the Goddess Al-Uzza.

But it is the story of the women of Petra, who fell from historical recognition that spark my interest. It is only recently that their value in the Nabatean society is now being pieced together. The Nabatean city of Petra was a strategic location which allowed the men to travel the world as traders, via the Silk Route that connected China to India and Egypt and the Incense Route from Arabia to Damascus, for most of the year leaving the women at home to rule the society. Petra thus became an influential commercial center with women holding positions of power. It was a Goddess worshipping cult with powerfully educated Priestesses who could not only read and write but who also held key roles in rituals as singers, musicians, and dancers. Here we have a clear example of ancient women not just of mythology, but reality, who had fallen from history only to be slowly unearthed now as to their correct magnitude.

We also have the very ancient and mysterious cult of the Essenes and the Dead Sea Scrolls. In the American clairvoyant Edgar Cayce's readings, he describes the women and men of the Essenes as equal. Most historical and biblical theologians focus more on the male members who were sometimes celibate, practiced piety towards the male God entity and lived within a communal setting while maintaining a pure lifestyle. Little is known of any Goddess or Priestess cult within the Essenes. New data being revealed has now stirred an ongoing debate about whether women were actually part of the largest Essenes settlement in Qumran, now an archaeological site located in the West Bank. Could they also have fallen from historical view?

"The literature also shows that women were excluded from all facets of public life. But a few narratives show women in positions of power."[1]

There are modern cultures in existence today that are not well-known but carry an ancient matrilineal societal line. They are somewhat obscure yet clearly holding onto the ancient traditions of the matriarch. These are women, in my opinion, who have drifted away from the norms of the patriarchal ethos. Historically these women have been deemed insignificant and thus were secreted away, yet within their cultures they have retained their supremacy.

One such obscure group are the Bribri of Costa Rico. A clan based indigenous people and a true matrilineal society. The clan heritage is defined by the female lineage with the women inheriting the land. Also, women hold important roles in the Bribri sacred rituals.

The Mosuo peoples of Tibet are another matrilineal society with lineage and property passing along the mother's line. Once again women take a leadership role in this culture and not only raise their children in the mother's household but also take the mother's name. Most importantly it is the Mosuo women who chose their partners and live separately. These are worthy examples of matriarchal societies that have survived. Though hidden, they do exist.

"At four million people, the Minangkabau of West Sumatra, Indonesia…are the largest known matrilineal society today."[2]

Here we have real equality within a society where couples have separate sleeping quarters and total separation of powers. True to ancient matriarchal cultures the mother is the most important person.

There are many other similar matriarchal civilizations of the present day such as the Khasi of India, Nagovisi of New Guinea, and the Akan peoples of Ghana. We are programmed to think of the patriarchal society that we now live in as the norm. These obscure matriarchal groups have not changed in over a millennium and beyond. World history does not celebrate these individuals, except as a curious specimen of antiquity. Thus, the women of these societies have vanished from their place in the historical narrative.

The men of these matrilineal cultures should be applauded for participating in a successful balance that has sustained a thriving family structure from the pages of antiquity to the reality of the present. The women within these societies are valued and not ignored.

There is currently a minor, yet crucial school of thought that believes when the Divine Feminine ruled across the ancient world creating highly functioning matrilineal societies, there was peace along with a unity of life that is sadly now missing.

Throughout ancient legends there is power in rediscovering the stories and experiences of the many women who have been dropped from the annals of history, plus those who are portrayed to us as enigmatic Goddesses, devout Saints, and repentant sinners. Modern women are walking a fresh avenue to wisdom as they acknowledge the past sufferings and joys of their ancestors and welcome the mystical holiness and power of their own bodies and minds.

I believe the few precious moments of freedom and knowledge felt by many of the *Fallen Women of Mythology* before the karmic axe fell on their memories was worth the journey. Forevermore identified as rebellious, scandalous, dark, or unimportant, these Goddesses, saints and sinners shook up the earliest biblical and cultural worlds with reverberations that to many modern thinkers, will hopefully be felt again today. I embrace their myths as a sacrosanct memorial to the Divine Feminine that was lost for a long time but has re-emerged as more intoxicating and powerful than ever.

Women have traditionally been written out of history. Here are stories of women, the hidden Goddesses of the ancient world. I want to awaken their voices. For within every account of a fallen woman whether Divine or human, there is another very fascinating side to their story.

Endnotes

1. https://jwa.org/encyclopedia/article/qumran
2. https://www.mentalfloss.com/article/31274/6-modern-societies-where-women-literally-rule

Chapter 1

The Sinners

It was an eye-opening moment to discover so many women of history, both real and mythological who were shoved into the perplexing category of sinner. Mainstream historians have given us a wealth of accounts about powerful women described as sinful because they were falsely labeled malevolent in their many varied roles as leaders and scholars; harlots and whores; herbalists and midwives or even fortunetellers. Perhaps that is why I am fascinated by unraveling their unique and individual stories. Since every beginning has an ending, the conclusion of many varied accounts of sinful women often resulted in the standard religious Christian trend of forgiveness and salvation with their ascension into sainthood or simple redemption. Moving away from certain Christian outcomes, we are left with women who never had the opportunity to reclaim their honor in their lifetimes. A few with the most dramatic stories were posthumously immortalized in art and literature. Thus, most of the fallen were forgotten and never remembered. Their false wickedness was never reprieved. To this day many still carry the naughty and broad label of sinner. Here was my dilemma in writing this book. Research has led me to many candidates who can claim the title of sinner or fit into the category of a fallen woman. Using the power of the word, I have chosen a diverse cross section of remarkable women with compelling stories. Some are obscure and others known, but all of their stories are worthy of our notice.

I believe it is a mutual historical consensus that these interpretations of women's lives stemmed from ancient religious scholars and historians' perspectives and not necessarily reality.

The influence of free-thinking women was a danger to society and the rule of the established hierarchy.

Women had worthwhile lives before and after being tagged as sinners. They deserve to be discovered anew and understood in a way that history did not, but that herstory will. To many their memories are a gateway to a renewed awareness of the inspiring role of real women who have found their way into the narrative of mythology.

How can one describe a "sinner" without a precise definition for the word "sin"? I believe that there are no clear meanings for this most ancient and troublesome word. The implications are multi-layered and vary according to the society, culture, and era. As a noun the word is explained as an immoral act or a transgression against God; an offense against the moral or religious laws of the society; a highly reprehensible act. As a verb it is defined as shame brought upon oneself becoming sinful and damned. Thus, to sin is to transgress against the divine laws interpreted by many varied religious societies and cultures. So, I shall express again and again in complete confidence within the pages of this book the following statement: the true meaning of "sin" is clearly seen in the eyes of the beholder.

Part I: Original Sinners

There is sin and then there is the "original sin." The author Augustine of Hippo 354–430 CE was the first to use the catchphrase "original sin". Since that time and until the present it has remained the well-known characterization of feminine historic disobedience that began in the Garden of Eden. Martin Luther and John Calvin, both Protestant reformers referred to original sin in more general terms, as hurtful desire with the loss of one's free will, with the sole purpose and desire to sin.

Within the many religious principles of the millennium there has been an abundance of different interpretations of sin, whether original or within life's transgressions. Morally different societies held different views on the belief of what constituted good or evil.

"In Judaism, it is believed that all humans enter the world free of sin. This makes the Jewish view of sin quite different from the Christian concept of original sin, in which it is believed that humans are tainted by sin from conception and must be redeemed through their faith. Jews believe that individuals are responsible for their own actions and that sin results when human inclinations go astray."[1]

There is no clear concept of sin in Buddhism as the belief centers around committing evil deeds that arrive from evil thoughts. The consequence of one's evil deeds and thoughts create suffering for the evil-doer as well as for those harmed.

In Japanese Shintoism the belief is that all human beings are born pure thus negating the concept of any type of original sin. In the Bahá'í Faith we are thought to be naturally good and essentially spiritual beings. With the concept of a mirror reflecting the human heart the only way to sin is to follow the penchant of one's inferior nature by turning the mirror away from God.

In ancient Greece hubris was defined as "excessive pride toward or defiance of the gods, leading to nemesis," was the ultimate sin in ancient Greece."[2]

The ancient mystic Jewish sect called the Essenes and owners of the Dead Sea Scrolls, defined sin as falling short, thus descending into our earthly bodies, and leaving our celestial flesh.

In the ancient tale of Oedipus, evil enters the heart in the form of arrogance and conceit and the Grecian gods show no mercy in their justice. For to sin in this way was the ultimate malevolence. Thus, the definition and the seriousness of the sin varied tremendously depending upon the act. The concept of sin has many guises as it continues to appear in one civilization after another.

At one time the Italian city of Venice held court to the lovely ladies of easy virtue who attracted visitors from all over the ancient world. The definition of sin is once again in the eyes of the beholder! As the stronghold of Christianity increased, accepted pleasure succumbed to sin but was nonetheless secretly welcomed and very profitable.

In our earliest records whether stone tablets or biblical text we have seen the feminine persona vilified again and again leading all the way to the present. Yet many of their stories were so often romanticized. One interesting analogy that I find pertinent is the Hollywood rendition of a sinful woman portrayed in the films of Greta Garbo. In one film entitled *Temptress* released in 1926, she is exactly that. She is beautiful and alluring and for that she is wickedly labeled. In the film *Romance,* released in 1930, there is one scene when Garbo says "I did nothing wrong". If looking beautiful is a sin, then she was a sinner. And that is how she is portrayed in each movie, loving freely, and looking fabulous!

Eve and Her Sister Lilith

Who are the female sinners of antiquity? One of the most famous women of sinful renown and biblically speaking, the first "original" sinner who fell from the celestial plains to the human world, was Eve. The need to impose punishment upon all womankind for Eve's supposed sinful act was necessary for the Christian sovereignty of the male order to succeed. Thus, the concept of collective guilt served the establishment well. In retrospect to most female sinners who are redeemed, Eve was never considered a penitent, thus she was never officially given sainthood or forgiveness from the ancient Christian hierarchy.

Whereas Eve was touted as the first sinner, her older sister Lilith really holds the title of being the first fallen woman. Lilith is often depicted as the cunning serpent who tempted Eve with the famous forbidden succulent apple at the Tree of Knowledge. Thus, the tale of so many fallen women is clearly mimicked in the following passage. Did Eve really feel the naïve pleasure in one bit of such a delectable fruit? Did she really commit an evil act of disobedience or simply a need to show her determined autonomy and passion.

The Book of Genesis tells Eve's story, but she does not fit the typical definition of a fallen woman who has sex outside of her marriage to Adam. She is expelled from the Garden of Eden for losing her innocence and her disobedience to Gods rules, after eating the forbidden fruit. But was that really the reason? Or was it because with that one act of defiance she gained more powerful knowledge than her male counterpart? Even with this harsh slander, the power of womankind and the Divine Feminine have survived.

Perhaps repentance insured acceptance through sainthood, but that was never a consideration for Lilith. Eve on the other hand, though never really forgiven, has several namesakes in the sainthood category such as Saint Eve of Dreux, Saint Eve of Liege, Eve of Saint-Martin, and Eve of Mount Cornelius. Adding insult to injury neither Lilith or Eve have been officially given the title of Goddess by the hierarchy of historical theologians or archeological scholars. But herstory does not ascribe to slander, instead it recognizes their divine connection to the sacred. If one is to interpret the quest for knowledge and the quest for independence as a sin then these are two very bad and rebellious fallen women. The need to suppress and silence women of antiquity was for me the real sin. I and many others of the same spiritual enlightenment prefer to see these women not as sinners or fallen but as role models for the ages.

Oddly enough I have found a vague and obscure reference that describes December 24th as a day to honor the Catholic personages Adam and the Matriarch Eve.

"It is perfect to remember today the sin of Adam and Eve that brought evil and corruption, suffering and death into God's perfect creation."[3]

Though obviously not practicing anymore, I was brought up as a strict Catholic who was very enamored by the tales of sainthood. It is very peculiar to my mind because I never remember celebrating the feast of Adam and Eve on Christmas Eve!

The English poet, John Milton, born in 1608 and died in1674, wrote the epic poem *Paradise Lost* which is his version of the biblical story of the temptation of Adam and Eve and their expulsion from the Garden of Eden. It is the saga of their utter fall from the Garden without any hope of forgiveness and the dire consequences that ensued. Through Milton's eyes the serpent in his poem becomes the fallen angel Satan. I ascribe to herstory whereby the serpent is Lilith and not an evil entity but an empowered Divine feminine influence who is a teacher of wisdom. And Lilith proudly never succumbed to becoming a reformed penitent either!

Thus, we have the fallen sinner Lilith, the most shadowy Biblical woman and to many a Goddess. She denied God's rules and was cast out of Eden because she would not lay beneath Adam, her supposed equally created partner. She teaches us the determination to be free from dominance and the power of liberation. Dear to my heart she also teaches us the power of passion and uninhibited pleasure which are powerfully empowering traits. Lilith begins her life in Eden co-existing with Adam. She then becomes the ultimate fallen woman. Within her story lies the carefully crafted deception that led to her bad press. From equal partner to feared demon, her story is a testament to the perpetual division between male and female. It is a story of the systematic tearing down of walls as day turns to night in the inevitable turn-about of power. Known as the fabled succubus of the Kabbalah and biblical renown she is the ultimate femme fatale and a timeless fallen woman.

Empress Wu

Though it is widely believed that the concept of "original sin" belongs to the Christian world, that is not entirely accurate. Another interpretation of women carrying the burden of an original sin makes a cruel appearance far from the Christian world, in ancient China. Women were considered inferior, simple chattel, a burden to society and a bad omen to their birth families. It was believed that a woman child inherited sin at her birth because she was not born a man. Since the role of women was so essential to birthing in a society, there had to be a way to use them effectively, yet control their character. That was attained by the strange and painful tradition of foot binding whereby a young girl's feet were tightly bound with cloth straps to prevent growth. This resulted in feet that were very deformed and small. Peasant women needed sticks for support to help them walk while the very wealthy were carried in a palanquin, a sort of carriage. This practice left women completely defenseless and crippled. Traditionally men of ancient China and traveling forward until the Chinese Revolution, when foot binding was finally outlawed, prized the hobbled feet and saw distorted legs as beautiful. I cannot use words to describe the horror that the visualization of this practice presents to my mind.

However, there were women who pursued and prospered in the arts and dance to make their mark in Chinese history despite this horrible hindrance. Though very little is known about them, there was one woman of great renown who ruled in the 7th century by the name of Empress Wu. She was a powerful Empress who ruled with an iron fist. History of the time was recorded by male scribes and they described her as an evil ruler who was accused of a murderous rampage upon her family. Were her real achievements hidden behind tiers of allegations? After all, Empress Wu was the first women in more than 3,000 years of Chinese history to rule in her own right despite the handicap of hobbled feet. Perhaps she was simply just a strong woman, trying to govern in a hostile world controlled by men. As with many other notorious women of antiquity she has been portrayed by historians and in movies and literature as a domineering and sexually aggressive woman. When she was old and at the end of her reign, historians claim she was relentless in her succession of erotic encounters with young men, Thus, Empress Wu was quite a woman. She was definitely characterized as an evil woman, and a sinful temptress, perhaps unfairly.

Mary Magdalene

Another femme fatale and well-known prostitute who began her journey as a sinner to become an infamous fallen woman of the ancient world was Mary Magdalene. She was demonized, shamed, and omitted from the Bible. In Christian thought Magdalene seeks salvation for her supposed sins of prostitution. But many herstorians now view her story as just another occurrence of bad press. Historically prostitutes of the ancient world were known as Magdelene's. Mary was a beautiful intelligent woman who was a sexual being, possibly a Temple Priestess, who was clearly and deliberately misunderstand by ancient male biblical theologians and scholars. For that she was branded a prostitute and sinner. The definition of fear is to be afraid; to sense danger or a threat. Is being an empowered woman really something to fear? Since history was written by men, they held the power to denigrate the female image. I do not think anyone seeing a so-called prostitute or a Priestess for that matter, really feels threatened. But it seems that our ancient theologians felt just that and crafted a very persuasive façade of evil around Magdalene.

There are many reasons why she needed to be brought down to fallen woman status. Her deep connection to Jesus for one, her influence and her powerful presence. I often wonder if she was the one with the ideas and inspiration. In ancient Hebrew tablets "Magdala" means tower. Perhaps she was the tower of wisdom who needed a male vehicle? As a woman she would never be accepted as a spiritual leader or teacher, so instead her partner Jesus became the face and the voice!

"Yet her real role as a spiritual leader was now over taken by her archetypal role as the redeemed 'fallen woman' whose repentance returns her to the control of the father. For the celibate male clergy focused on disempowering women, this put her in a manageable place, at the feet of Jesus—and all men—where she could be tamed."[4]

Although there has been an incredible amount of provocative literature and art about Mary Magdalene, it is still important to add her to the list of sinful fallen women of mythology. What was her authentic self?

"Although the Bible does not tell us the origins of Mary Magdalene, she bears all the hallmarks of an empowered priestess and of a prophetess of the Goddess traditions."[5]

Was she just a misunderstood Priestess and perhaps a wife, who was unfairly identified as a sinner? Did Jesus really drive out seven demons from her soul? Was she a Sacred Prostitute? Did she participate in "holy matrimony" with Jesus? In ancient texts and book after book plus numerous plays and movies she is portrayed as all of the above. Nonetheless, she fell at the beginning of her inception in veiled ancient texts.

A Prostitute is defined as a woman who has become a moral degenerate and sinner because she has lost her chastity or honor. Touted as a sinner and prostitute Magdalene slowly works her way clear in the eyes of scriptural authors and theologians. One way she accomplishes this is by becoming a disciple of Jesus along with her humbling act of washing his feet, the intimate act of drying them with her luxurious hair and anointing them with fragrant oils. Perhaps not just an unpretentious act but also one of familiar sensuality. Bending down with her abundant hair touching his feet like soft feathers creates a visual that is not modest. Thus, the sinner began to redeem herself. Historically speaking she repents and is forgiven and the Christian world now recognizes her as a Saint. Saint Mary Magdalene, from sinner to fallen woman to sainthood and beloved by many.

Most theologians see sacred prostitutes who channeled the power of Divinity as fallen women. Still the ancient Pharaohs, Emperors, and Kings acting as willing participants in sexual acts with a Priestess as a sacred prostitute were never labelled with a similar fallen identity. Male hierarchy welcomed the powerful act because it confirmed that he was a recipient of celestial or divine power bestowed upon him by the holy copulation.

Divine Sophia

Was Mary Magdalene and too many other ancient women considered fallen simply because they displayed unapologetic and/or commanding traits. Like Lilith and Magdalene comes a mythological story of yet another misunderstood deity, one who began as the womb of creation and one that suddenly dropped to the status of a fallen woman. How, when, and why?

Sophia, whose name means "wisdom" in multiple religious and cultural traditions, is a complex holy figure described variously as a divine element, a Goddess, a co-partner or even equal to God as a contrast between his dual human and divine nature. She was thought by many to be the multi-dimensional feminine beginning, the spark within the womb of the cosmos. From the foundation of time her essence has been in the conscious mind of many and the subconscious of most. And from Gnostic mysticism to Hellenistic philosophy Sophia appears as essential to the creation of the universe and as the Universal Mother she is called "love." But within her complex story she ultimately falls hard.

Within Gnostic texts, ancient Jewish tradition, and also in early Christian writings, Sophia is described as the Creatrix, and Celestial Goddess of Wisdom. The Gnostics call her the feminine Face of God. While other scholars associate her with the Egyptian Goddesses Maat and Isis plus the Greek Goddesses Demeter, Persephone, Hecate, and Ishtar, the Mesopotamian Goddess of Love. She is an enigma and her origins defy definition because her power is rooted in her divine wisdom.

"Scholars have dated Sophia's textual sources at least 500 years after most of the Hebrew tradition was developed. Sophia can be found in The Book of Proverbs, Wisdom of Solomon, Ecclesiasticus (Ben Sirach), and in the Christian Gospels and epistles."[6]

As her story reveals, as a Goddess and a Divine source, her growing influence threatened the patriarchal establishment and like the disobedient Eve, she falls swiftly. In Gnostic texts Sophia succumbs to a defiant and sinful act. She wanted to have a child, but she went about it the wrong way. She did not involve her partner nor did she get the approval of the Father God. The result is her giving birth to the demiurge, a distorted creature unlike other heavenly beings. Regretting, her action, Sophia then casts away her child out of the Pleroma, the spiritual universe within the totality of the divine power. Alone and foolishly ignorant, the demiurge creates the material world. Sophia is then forced by her action to become an imperfect being. She is compelled to move away from the perfect fullness of the Pleroma and the Divinity of the spiritual world into the materialistic world of humanity, just like Eve. Ancient texts then tell the story of Sophia's repentance and that God the Father brings her back to the Pleroma. Once thought to be the first Feminine principal, the Divine Goddess Sophia falls from grace to be labelled a sinner because of one rebellious action. Her story is not just of a sinful act, but it is more about repentance when she is punished and thrown from the light into the darkness of the physical world, until she is redeemed by her possible consort, the God. Beyond her story of sin and redemption, in many early devout Christian writings Sophia continues to be regarded as a true female representation of Christ. And it is within the Roman Catholic and Eastern Orthodoxy traditions that she is eventually restored to her proper place in Divinity when she was canonized as a Saint.

The ancient Byzantine empire dedicated a church, the Hagia Sophia, which means the Holy Wisdom to the memory of the Divine Sophia. Thus, Sophia morphs from a sinful Goddess to becoming Saint Sophia sometimes referred to as the third person of the trinity, the Father, son, and herself as the feminine Holy Spirit. Let us not confuse her with another Saint Sophia, the Eastern Orthodox Church's martyr, along with her three daughter's Faith, Hope, and Love.

"Veneration of the goddess continued as part of Christianity in groups such as Cathars, Essenes, Templars, Gnostics, Rosicrucians, and Celtic Christians."[7]

"As Goddess of wisdom and fate, her faces are many: Black Goddess, Divine Feminine, Mother of God, To Gnostic Christians, Sophia was the Mother of Creation; her consort and assistant was Jehovah. Her sacred shrine, Hagia Sophia in Istanbul, is one of the seven wonders of the world. Her symbol, the dove, represents spirit; she is crowned by stars, a Middle Eastern icon, to indicate her absolute divinity."[8]

Sophia is the ultimate incarnation of Sacred Wisdom and for many the Goddess who inspires all. In Christian theology she forms a connection with the Holy Spirit. In Rosicrucian tradition Sophia is placed in the higher realm on the Tree of life.

> "In Proverbs 8, Sophia speaks of herself. She was with God before creation, and she was the master worker through whom God created (see especially 8:22-31). In Sirach 24, she is from eternity and fills all that is. In the Wisdom of Solomon 7:22-27, she is "the fashioner" and "mother" of all good things..."[9]

There is no end to the many variations of Sophia's name. To the Greeks she meant wisdom. The Aramaic word "hayat" describes her as one who gives birth to life and to the Navajo, she was Spider Woman or Changing Woman.

> "Gnostics today have reverential names for the earth mother: the Aeon Sophia, or the Aeonic Mother, the Divine Mother, World Mother or simply PAM, Planetary Animal Mother."[10]

Sophia is a revered spiritual star and to love her is to love life. From Goddess to sinner to Saint and Goddess again, Sophia was and still is to many of us, the illumination of the Solar Mother. Perhaps her light was simply too bright.

In referencing the image of the Goddess Sophia as crowned by stars, I am reminded of St. Mary, the Virgin Mother of Jesus, and a Catholic prayer that begins *O'Mary crowned with stars...* and ancient depictions of the Goddess Isis with a crown of stars circling her head. One cannot think of these connections without seeing the Goddess everywhere in the mythologies of the Divine Feminine and in the souls of all women who have experienced struggles and victories.

"I am she who was, and is, and shall be. No man has lifted my veil."[11]

Part II: Sinful Luminaries
Jeanne D'Arc

One of the most famous female leaders who regretfully fell from grace was Saint Jeanne D'Arc. She became a luminary when she began to receive her prophetic visions in 1425 at the age of only 13, where she beheld St. Michael, St. Catherine of Alexandria, and St. Margaret of Antioch. These visions convinced her to seek an audience with the uncrowned King Charles VII of France. In this meeting she claimed God himself gave her not only the visions but instructed her to re-claim France's sovereignty from Britain and their occupying Burgundian allies. With her successful liberation of France in 1430 she became infamous.

"Sadly, her magnetic leadership and her divine visions became interpretated negatively by the anxious clergy hierarchy who were threatened by her strong appeal. What followed was persecution by both church and state in her Inquisitorial trial, and her ultimate execution. It is no surprise that she is eventually redeemed by being made into a Christian Saint."[12]

Her sinful rehabilitation was complete in 1909 when she was beatified by Pope Pius X and was subsequently canonized in 1929 by Pope Benedict XV to become St. Joan.

Queen Kubaba

There were many female rulers and leaders in antiquity, some well-known and others almost forgotten. One such ruler was Queen Kubaba of Sumer, now Iraq. She ruled around 2,400 BC. Very little is known about her except that she was thought to be the first ever recorded queen in history and the only queen listed on the Sumerian Kings list. Some versions of her story place her as a ruler in either the 3rd or 4th dynasty while parts of her mythos compare her to a Goddess. She was not a sinner or saint or a fallen woman, yet it is vital to acknowledge her value. Regretfully her full legend as a luminary has been lost to mainstream history.

Hatshepsut, Pharoah of Egypt

Another ancient ruler was the daughter of the 18th Dynasty Pharaoh Thutmose I, who was born almost 3,500 years ago in Egypt. Her name was Hatshepsut and she was married to her half-brother, Thutmose II. Upon his death she acted as regent for his infant son, Thutmose III, born by another consort. This continued for a number of years, with both acting as co-rulers.

During these years the portrait depictions of Hatshepsut show her in the appropriate feminine body and garments. In the 7th year of Thutmose III's rule, Hatshepsut adopted the full authority as Pharaoh of Egypt. Now her official portraits suddenly began to combine a female body with kingly regalia. Ultimately, she is shown with a male body, false beard, and crown. She was part of a male dominated society and she morphed into the image that was acceptable and would insure her claim to kingship. She was a dominant ruler who surrounded herself with a loyal group of government officials. One figure who history claims might have been her lover was Senenmut, overseer of all royal works, a most influential post.

As Pharoah, Hatshepsut was more interested in peace and foreign trade rather than war. She re-established the trade routes disrupted by the Hyksos occupation of Egypt, thereby insuring the wealth of the 18th Dynasty. She also embarked upon restoration projects and a tremendous new building program. During her reign she remodeled part of the temple complex at Karnak, built a rock-cut temple at Beni Hasan, a funerary monument designed as a temple for herself at Dayr al Bahri and the granite obelisk that is now known as the Hatshepsut needle. Reigning from around 1473 to 1458 BCE, she had attained unprecedented power for a woman.

Hatshepsut was not a sinner or saint, nor did she morph into a Goddess persona, but a woman who had surely fallen in the eyes of the hierarchy. She was a woman of antiquity whose true worth was somewhat weakened and lost by historians and archeologists who portrayed her as a woman placed in power by males to further their own wealth. The mistaken thought among historians was that her reign in the early years was simply a placeholder to serve her father Thutmose I who was away on a military campaign. Another theory was that she was just a prominent High Priestess.

At the end of her reign Hatshepsut released power to Thutmose III who ruled for another 33 years. Sadly, after her death with the destruction of her statutes and monuments her name was almost entirely removed, thus she disappeared from the official kings list. This act of revenge ensured the male succession from Thutmose I though Thutmose II to Thutmose III without female interruption. Hatshepsut had fallen from the pages of history. Her legacy was lost until 1822 when archeologists decoded hieroglyphic scripts that suddenly explained the inconsistency between the female name and the male likeness that had caused such confusion. Fallen no longer and a genuine luminary, we can now admire the reign of Hatshepsut who was indeed a great female Pharaoh. Hatshepsut and her father Thutmose I were buried together in the Valley of the Kings.

Boudica, Queen of the Celts

Traveling to the time of the Celtic Britons we have Queen Boudica of the Iceni Tribe, who in 60 or 61 BCE led a rebellion against the conquering forces of the Roman Empire. Touted for her bravery she was also known as a rebellious heroine or as some not so favorable historians describe, a cruel and merciless fighter. She was a symbol of the struggle for justice and independence. Her people were grossly mistreated as slaves of the Romans and she was known to be ruthless in her revenge. Regretfully, the rebellion failed and it was thought that Boudica either poisoned herself or died of her battleground wounds, yet there is no clear evidence of either fate.

Cassius Dio wrote that she was very tall and had a frightening appearance with dark yellow hair that hung below her waist with a piercing voice and harsh glare. He describes her clothing as colorful tunics surrounded by thick cloaks held together by a gold brooch. Around her neck she wore a golden torc which was a thick heavy choker necklace. I find it very interesting that Cassius Dio was a Roman historian from the period 155 to 235 CE, and also a senator of maternal Greek origin. He obviously wrote many years after the rebellion, perhaps with the bias held by many male historians against a powerful female leader.

Boudica is so often portrayed as being too frightening and sinfully cruel to her enemies. Her imposing presence should be redefined as a powerful virtue of salvation for her people against their repressive enemies. In retrospect she has become almost a mythological heroine who is virtually considered the nearest to a Goddess persona with the Celtic peoples.

Olympias, Queen of Macedonia

Another under rated luminary was the mother of Alexander the Great. During her reign, really a co-regency, as Queen of Macedonia, she was described as a violent and ambitious ruler. Her name was Olympias and she was born in 375 BCE, the daughter of Neoptolemus I of Epirus, a Greek king. Her marriage to King Phillip II of Greece was a political alliance and although it was a tumultuous marriage, she bore Philip a daughter and a son, Alexander. A fascinating woman who various scholars believe was a snake handler and who belonged to the Cult of Dionysus. Dionysus was the son of the Greek

Goddess Demeter and the God Zeus. His cults beliefs formed around the worship of fertility and wine culminating in the fervor of religious ecstasy.

With Alexander as the heir presumptive, she touted within Court circles that he was not really Phillip's son, but actually the son of Zeus thus having a divine origin. Upon the death of her husband and Alexander's ascension to the throne she gained even more power. Phillip was said to have been assassinated and the blame was thrust upon Olympias and Alexander. Now with Alexander on the throne but so often away, Olympias felt she needed to protect his interests by whatever means were within her grasp. Historians write of sinister acts, of court intrigues, poisonings, and murders with her as the culpable person. With the death of Alexander, she tried to maintain her powerful hold but was ultimately stoned to death by the relatives of her victims upon orders from her stepson Cassander.

Olympias was perhaps a sinful woman and even a seductress if one ascribes to the conventional historical views. However, she was a Mother and a Queen who helped her son maintain his kingdom as he continuously conquered new territories from Greece to India.

Interestingly, in 2019 during excavations in the Tomb of Korinos in Northern Greece, Emeritus Professor Athanasios Bidas read a set of inscriptions that led him to identify a tomb that was a smaller version of Alexander the Great's Tomb.

"A *Greek Times* article says the archaeologists at the site asked themselves "what person could such a huge idiosyncratic monument be built other than for the mother of Alexander the Great?," the professor told reporters."[13]

Cleopatra

Too many powerful female leaders of antiquity were defiled by historians into being portrayed as not only sinful but, disappointing. Cleopatra VII, from the late 1st century BCE, was one of the best-known leaders in Egyptian history who was regretfully marked as just a true sinful luminary and a succubus. History falsely records that her power was only in her beauty and not in her intelligence. Herstory sees her differently. She was a leader who defied the rules made by the male hierarchy by not letting any man or army stand in her way. She knew how to manipulate her power to keep control of all of Egypt's land. She captured the hearts of Caesar and Marc Antony, the two most illustrious and powerful men of their time.

She was a ruler in a time of Rome's heightened power and Egypt was the ultimate prize. She kept Egypt whole for as long as possible even under the most volatile circumstances, more than any male pharaoh could have done. The alure of her legacy has survived from works of art and literature to silent films and Hollywood blockbusters. She has become a contemporary cultural icon. Nonetheless history has maliciously labelled her a fallen woman and a symbol of the ultimate femme fatale who regretfully lost her empire.

Catherine the Great

Another famous leader who shared some of Cleopatra's traits, was falsely maligned as an insanely driven femme fatal. Here name was Catherine the Great. She was married at a young age to a Russian prince who became the Emperor of Russia, with Catherine as his Empress. She was born Sophie of Anhalt-Zerbst on May 2, 1729 in Stettin, Province of Pomerania, Kingdom of Prussia, the Holy Roman Empire, as Princess Sophie Friederike Auguste von Anhalt-Zerbst-Dornburg. She died on November 17, 1796. Though not a ruler in the early days of antiquity, she did govern Russia as the last Empress Regnant almost 300 hundred years ago and her image as a sinful woman is pertinent to this book. As her story goes, with the support of Russia's generals, admirals, and the military she was able to lead a successful coup to overthrow her weak and ineffective husband Peter III. Catherine grabbed the reins of power at a time in Russia's history when the country was expanding with one conquest after another. She modernized the government and ushered in a cultural renaissance of art and education within the Empire. She was a strong and manipulative politician, who used her feminine powers to the fullest extent to achieve her goals. It is because of such behavior that she was misunderstood by historians. She has become famous over the years since her reign ended for being an unbridled succubus who took vital lovers and had liaisons to further her bidding. But what if she did, it does not diminish her power as a leader. Catherine was not Russian but she loved the Russian people and under her rule left a lasting mark of culture, education, and prosperity in Russia. Despite any falsehoods about her person, historians have bestowed upon her the title of Catherine the Great.

Lucrezia Borgia

When researching sinful woman of power and influence one cannot ignore the infamous Lucrezia Borgia who was branded not only as a sinful femme fatale who was guilty of incest, but also a poisoner and murderess. She was a Valencian woman born in 1480 and died in 1519. The timeline of her life is filled with well documented bad behavior. But Lucrezia had little to no control of her life. She was thrown against her will into one marriage and affair after another. She was truly used as a political pawn by the papal male hierarchy of the powerful ruling Borgia family.

She was the daughter of Pope Alexander VI and was described as a beautiful woman with long thick blonde hair, fair complexion and hazel eyes. She was an artist's dream who seemed to walk on air with her natural grace. And indeed, her lovely image has been portrayed in paintings, sculptures and in literature for centuries.

The wealthy Borgia dynasty ruled the papal court, with lust and intrigue, so much for the piety of the Catholic Church! The Borgia's were a family of hereditary Popes who discarded their vows of celibacy and modesty during their brutal rein. Lucrezia's survival was a calculated balance between her desires and the betrayal of the papal court. But history is never understanding or fair!

Lucrezia Borgia was not an artist's model but her ethereal beauty and alluring dark side was a favorite subject for artists throughout the centuries who romanticized her image from a dangerous succubus to a captivating and luminous Medieval fallen lady.

Part III: Sins of the Flesh
Artist Models

We need only to look at thousands of years of religious sculptures, paintings, and drawings to see the fascination and appreciation of the female form which inspired artists to create some of the world's most beautiful works of art. So, who is the sinner here, the model, the artist or patron, or Christendom for soliciting such works? With Eve and Adam's banishment from the Garden Paradise called Eden, they suddenly experienced the feeling of shame and the body became covered. Since sin supposedly originated with Eve in the bible, it was thought to be sinful to display too much of the female form. But in Churches and Cathedrals stretching from the Vatican and Rome to the far reaches of the world, nudity covers the ceilings and walls from sensual angels and seductive nymphs to pious and slightly clad saints plus a vast array of biblical figures and Goddesses. Though many try, one cannot decipher or unravel the real meaning of the sin of nudity, for it is an enigma.

Throughout history many female models, both famous and unknown, posed for artists who painted mystifying images like the Italian artist Leonardo da Vinci's demure *Mona Lisa* in

1503, to the Italian painter Botticelli's the *Birth of Venus* in the 1480's to the tantalizing naked body of La Morphise painted by the French painter François Boucher around 1753. Marie-Louise O' Murphy, who was known as La Morphise, was the provocative nymph who graced King Louis XV's palace ceiling. Though she was a lessor mistress of the King, her seductive body has become immortalized. These female images are so magnificent that they have become part of mythology in their origins.

In a complete turn about, the women whose graceful female forms were so admired in art and desired in life were judged, and in many instances criminalized by society as wicked fallen women, immoral and sinful. What a conundrum! In Paris in the 1600's modelling was a criminal offense yet during that period we have a vast array of art that was produced with the female form in all its many aspects. And the famous French Academie School held life drawing classes, with nude models, during this period of criminality. There was a model during this period by the name of Anon who supposedly wrote a diary of her journey to become a model. Though her diary was never authenticated it is interesting to read about her dealings with contentious and overly talented and temperamental artists.

Phryne

"The first professional model we know anything about was Phryne who lived in Athens in the fourth century BC."[14]

During this period of antiquity models were considered almost as important as the artist. Phryne posed for the famous statute *Aphrodite of Knidos* created by the artist Praxiteles of Athens. This statute was the first life size image of the nude female form in Greek history and shifted the previous trend of male bodies to that of the superb female figure. Though Phryne was famously portraited as a Deity by Praxiteles, she was really known as a desired courtesan who Greek society considered a second-class citizen. She was criticized for her ability to seduce her male admirers for financial gain. Was she sinful?

Zafetta

The famous Venetian painter Titian painted the *Venus of Urbino* possibly using the little-known courtesan named Zafetta as his model. There lays the Goddess in all her glory reclining so candidly and without shame on a sofa. It is a likeness that has been copied by many artists of the time including another Venetian painter by the name of Giorgione whose stunning *Dresden Venus* follows a similar style. The seductive reclining Goddess became a recurring theme in classical art in both sculpture and painting. Considered fallen women by the social order of the time, their identities seemed unimportant to conventional art historians. The images of these little-known courtesans and models have given us the most amazing representations of the classical female form venerated for centuries in Palaces, Museums, Galleries, Cathedrals, and Churches throughout the world. Their stories need a voice so they can be remembered, without lifestyle prejudice, for their incredible contributions to art history through the ages.

La Dame aux Camelias

One of the most famous courtesans of the 19th century was Maria Duplessis, known as La Dame aux Camelias. She was the lover of the French writer Alexandre Dumas who wrote his famous semi auto-biographical novel entitled *La Dame aux Camelias* about his real-life affair with Maria. She was portrayed as the fictional very young delicate courtesan named Marguerite Gautier, suffering from consumption with Alexandre as Armand Duval her young bourgeois lover.

Dumas' book has been adapted for stage and screen around the world. The coveted role of the fallen woman Marguerite

Gautier has been played by Sarah Bernhardt, Lillian Gish, Theda Bara, Greta Garbo, Francesca Bertini, Isabelle Huppert, and many others.

There is a marvelous portrait of the real-life Maria Duplessis painted by the French artist Edouard Vienot which not only shows her mesmerizing and exquisite beauty but her trademark white Camilla bloom at her bosom. Though famous for the love of her many paramours she was nonetheless considered a sinful and fallen woman.

Elizabeth Siddell

One more important artistic movement that welcomed the artist model had turned away from the classical to embrace the British Pre-Raphaelite movement of the 1850's, and the Symbolist Movement of the 1890's. Or in more common terms, the Art Nouveau movement. Artists began a quest for an unconscious dreamlike quality in their works. And the models mirrored their visions. Models were often shared and very often because of the decadence of the time experimented with opiates such as laudanum and choral to achieve the solemn look required by the artists.

Elizabeth Siddell was one such model who ended her days in an opiate trance along with consumption. Yet she was a devoted model who posed for John Everett Millais as the drowning "Ophelia." Elizabeth laying on her back fully dressed in a soaked velvet and brocade gown did not mention to Millais that the heating lamp under the bath had gone out. Mesmerized by her role and not wanting to disturb his creative process, she lay uncomplaining for five hours until totally frozen. She was an ethereal creature who was paid the common model rate of seven shillings per day. Being that she was a favorite amongst artists of the period such as Dante Gabriel Rossetti and Holman Hunt, Elizabeth would pose for two or three artists at the same time.

Elizabeth ultimately accepted a marriage proposal from Rossetti late in her career. She died at the age of 33. Here is an intimate report that really verbalizes the somber fascination that attracted Rossetti to her.

"He loved her best when after a dose she layed in her armchair and acted dead."[15]

The scandalous women models of the decadent late 1800's left their mark on the art of the period. Society was beginning to break out of its Victorian repression, nevertheless these sinful fallen women were scorned by normal society. Often unmarried and living with various artists and left to find comfort in the dreamlike stupor of readily available opiates.

I was an artist's model for many years, during my dance career, posing at the Art Students League and Parsons in New York City. I was known for my long poses, one of which was my favorite, the reclining Goddess. One teacher remarked that I lay as still as death, little did he know that I was channeling my model ancestors in out of body moments. Sometimes I felt I was channeling Elizabeth Siddell, without the opiates, as she lay for *Ophelia.* I do not know if any works of art that featured my form ever became known but it was a deeply profound experience to finish a pose and to view the artists progress in the creation of their work. And I do not consider myself fallen or sinful! The immoral artist's model so often seen and admired but never heard. Almost mythological in their visual legacy.

Part IV: The Witches

The *Malleus Maleficarum*, known as the Hammer of Witches was written in the 15th century and is the well-known discourse about Witchcraft or at least what was thought of at that time. It was the *Malleus* that suggested torture to get confessions which caused the need to kill the evils of witchcraft.

How can I bring to life women of fallen reality and mythology who have not fared well with the ancient press without bringing us a hundred years forward to the Witch Trials of Salem, Massachusetts in 1692. It was not only women, men were also were accused, tortured, tried, and put to death under false allegations. They were all wrongly labeled as sinners against God in this heinous miscarriage of justice. Rumors of flying on brooms, naked encounters in the forest late on moonlight nights to rendezvous with the horned God or Devil, plus doing spells and casting curses were only part of the completely prejudicial and unfounded crimes.

Thirty innocent individuals were found guilty, nineteen were executed by hanging, fourteen women and five men. One man Giles Corey was pressed to death by stones; and at least five people died in prison. It was a sad episode of mass hysteria in the early history of this colonial New World. The restrictive Puritan lifestyle, religious fervor, jealousy, the terror of deadly influenza combined with the isolation of many, created a breeding ground for fear and superstition that lead up to this horrific event. And the hysteria reached beyond Salem Village and the surrounding towns. Well before the Salem trials Europe went through a more deadly phenomenon of Witch torture and trials. Though not supported by clear evidence, many scholars and historians estimate the Burning Times, lasted from 600 until 1700, possibly a period of 1,100 years. Mostly women, as widows, elderly or midwives were charged with heresy and other unsubstantiated crimes and were hanged or burned at the stake. The astronomical numbers of women accused in many instances wiped out the female populations of entire villages which ultimately forced the persecution to decline. There are estimates ranging from tens of thousands to millions of people, mostly women, who were tortured and put to death.

The mind set of the time of the great burning was to further the power of the male hierarchy and thus women were disposable.

One of the first recorded Witchcraft trials in the Colonies of the New World was in Windsor, Connecticut in 1647 when Alse Young was accused of Witchcraft and hanged. Alie Beamon her one female child was also condemned for the same crime of Witchcraft in the 1670's, thirty years after her mother's hanging. Luckily Alie was not hanged. The inability to understand disease and with little access to medical care it was easier to point a finger at someone as the cause. Sadly, Alse, Alie's mother, was probably that person.

Salem Witches

In the last three hundred years there have been numerous accounts and written documentation about the Salem Witch Trials in Massachusetts in 1692. It was two young girls who started the whirl wind of crazy and false accusations hurled at various women in Salem Village, causing a terrifying time when neighbor was pitted against neighbor. Though some of the names of the accused women have become well known, it is vital to relive their stories again and again as a reminder of injustice.

The first woman executed was 71-year-old Rebeca Nurse who was arrested on March 24, 1692 and hanged on July 19, 1962. Rebecca was also a pious woman and a well-respected member of the community. Never repenting because she believed firmly that she was innocent. Surely too late, she was fully exonerated 20 years later.

Another of the first women to be accused at the Salem Witch Trials on February 29, 1692 was Sarah Good. She was one of the youngest and pregnant at the time of her accusation. As a daughter of a successful tavern owner, she was hanged on July 19, 1692. Her infant daughter who was born to her while imprisoned sadly died before her mother was hanged. Though it was little compensation too late, in 1710 damages in the amount of thirty pounds sterling was granted to Sarah's family by the lawyer William Good who sued the Great and General Court on her behalf. Though it was a large sum at the time it was little reparation for the damage done to the Good family and for the victim's descendants.

Sarah Osborne was yet another of the women arrested on February 29, 1692. Sadly, she was accused by a fellow prisoner, Sarah Good, and even more regretfully she also died before her trial in a Boston prison on May 10, 1692. She was only in her 40's. Though never officially exonerated, she was part of the memorial dedication by Salem Village Witchcraft Victims' Memorial of Danvers on May 9, 1992.

Martha Corey was the wife of Giles Coey, who was also arrested, tortured, and killed under the weight of heavy stones. Martha was a woman in her 70's, when she was arrested on March 21, 1692. She was to become the last woman hanged on September 22, 1692. She was an official member of the Salem Village Church since 1661 and was thought to be a pious woman who attended church regularly. In 1703 the Salem Church revoked her excommunication and in 1711 the Province of Massachusetts Bay restored her innocence.

Mary Easty, a 56-year-old, woman was arrested on rumors and allegations made by the Gould family, in anger over her defense of Rev. Thomas Gilbert with whom the Gould family held a grudge. She was arrested on April 21, 1962, she was released on May 18, 1692. Sadly, she was re-arrested on May 20, 1692 and was finally executed by hanging on September 22, 1692. Mary was the wife of a wealthy Topsfield farmer and was also the sister of Rebeca Nurse. She was exonerated in 1711 and her descendants' received restitution of 20 pounds.

Sarah Wildes was also arrested on April 21, 1692 and executed by hanging on July 19, 1692. She was a 65-year-old resident of Topsfield and related to both the Gould and Putnam families whose feud fueled so many of the false allegations. Years later she was proved innocent with relatives receiving restitution by the Massachusetts General Court in 1710. She joined others who were accused being cleared by an act of Legislature on October 31, 2001.

Lydia Dustin a woman in her mid-60's was arrested on April 30, 1692 and sadly died in prison on March 10, 1693. She was not even a resident of Salem Village, but the neighboring town of Reading. She was a widow whose husband had been one of the leading landowners in Reading. Although she was acquitted, she was held in prison because she could not pay the fines. In time she was ultimately cleared.

Susannah Martin was a baptized and known pious church member. She was a 71-year-old resident of Amesbury and was arrested on May 2, 1692. As with many others accused, Susannah pleaded not guilty to her crimes. Sadly, with Cotton Mather Witch hunter and Puritan clergyman in charge she was not allowed to have counsel. Thus, she was hanged on July 19, 1692. She was not exonerated until October 31, 2001 by the Commonwealth of Massachusetts!

Alice Parker who was a resident of Salem Town. Accused of multiple crimes including casting spells, bewitching and murder, was arrested on May 12, 1692. Though she joined others in profusely proclaiming her innocence, she was hanged on September 22, 1692. She was also exonerated on October 31, 2001 by the Commonwealth of Massachusetts.

Ann Pudeator was another resident of Salem Town. Records show that she was probably a nurse and midwife which made her particularly prone to accusations. Thus, she was arrested on May 12, 1692 and at the age of 70 and was hanged on September 22, 1692. Her conviction was reversed in 1710.

Margaret Scott was a 77-year-old resident of Rowley and a very poor widow. Because of her degraded circumstances she was forced to beg and thus she became an obvious candidate for slander and suspicion. She was arrested around August 5, 1692 and hanged on September 22, 1692. Like so many of her fellow accused she exclaimed her innocence to no avail. She was also exonerated on October 31, 2001.

Elizabeth How a woman in her 50's was a resident of Topsfield when she was arrested on May 29, 1692. She more than any other accused had a large number of loyal fiends who came to her defense during her trial. But due to spectral evidence which was believed, she was found guilty and was hanged on July 19, 1692. She left behind six children and a blind husband. Thanks to the diligence of one of her daughters Elizabeth, she joined the list of others whose convictions were reversed and nullified in 1711.

Ann Foster another widowed woman of crone age was a resident of Andover. She was arrested on July 15, 1692 and died in prison on December 2, 1692. She along with others was exonerated in 1711 by the Province of Massachusetts Bay.

Mary Parker was a 55-year-old widow and a resident of Andover. She was arrested around September 2, 1692 and hanged with many others on September 22, 1692. Her daughter Alice Parker sadly joined her. She was exonerated between 1710 and 1711 with relatives claiming restitution.

Among the nearly 200 women who were arrested during the Salem Witch trials one woman was miraculously saved from hanging at the final moment when the Puritanical fever began to dissipate. Her name was Elizabeth Johnson and she was only 22 years old. She was spared and then completely forgotten. Many of her fellow defendants were eventually acquitted when the officials of the time and in the future began to understand the injuries bestowed upon those accused by their sham and unjust charges. But Elizabeth was somehow forgotten and lost until very recently when modern lawmakers realized their omission and remedied the situation by acquitting her.

"Lawmakers agreed to reconsider her case last year after a curious eighth-grade civics class at North Andover Middle School took up her cause and researched the legislative steps needed to clear her name."[16]

She was pardoned and finally released from her supposed sin and her memory liberated. Many fallen women who were completely innocent were finally redeemed!

Marie Laveau, Queen of Voodoo

Marie Laveau a mesmerizing and mysterious Louisiana Creole was the Queen of Voodoo in the New Orleans area. Marie Catherine Laveau was born in 1801 and died in 1881. She was many things including an herbalist, midwife, conjurer, and root worker. But she was best known for her practice of Voodoo. People hear the word Voodoo and immediately think the worst. But Maria was known for her care of the sick and needy. She mixed herbal remedies and prayers for the afflicted during the yellow fever epidemic of 1878. She also performed rituals to help those in need and she never charged them for her services. She was a sought-after Voodoo Queen who helped with family disputes, health, finance, and love. The historical press acknowledged that she was a powerful practitioner of Voodoo, which is considered one of the dark arts and for that she was branded with trepidation and foreboding. Voodoo is ja mix of ancient beliefs and rituals using herbs and a bit of sorcery that combines Haitian and Caribbean folklore with traditional Roman Catholic saints and rituals. Marie also combined her practice of Native American spiritualism and African spirits to create her unique roots in Louisiana Voodoo.

She was an influential and strong female spiritual leader who was also known to continue her strong ties and devotion to the Catholic faith by receiving communion. It was said that she had a snake named Zombi which she probably used as her familiar and guide in some of her communications with the spirit world. Snakes are powerful symbols of eternity, wisdom, and transformation. Voodoo Priestesses pray to their saints and contact the spirit realm to receive information. Though different in their techniques Trance Mediums also commune with the dead to receive messages. Marie's legacy is that she used Voodoo, adding her distinctive combination of spiritual practices to help people. Sadly, historians continue to weave a web of fear and negative misunderstanding around her memory. Her grave lays in St. Louis Cemetery in New Orleans and is constantly visited by hundreds of devoted follows who leave offerings in her honor to this day.

Rebecca Yorke

One last interesting story about a so-called fallen women was Jane Rebecca Yorke of the United Kingdom, who was known for being one of Britian's last convicted Witches in 1944. Jane worked as a medium for many years in Forest Gate, Essex, before being prosecuted under the 209-year-old Witchcraft Act. She was accused of defrauding the public by exploiting wartime fears and was tried in London's Central Criminal Court. Because she was 72 years old, Jane was only given a fine of five pounds and a probation period of three years.

Just a few years later, in 1951, the United Kingdom officially opened the doors to Witches by repealing the Witchcraft Act with the enactment of the Fraudulent Mediums Act.

In the United States every individual state has their own laws and jurisdiction regarding tarot readings and other forms of fortunetelling, some still very active. The District Court of Virginia recognized Witchcraft as a legitimate religion in the 1980's. Ultimately upheld by a Federal Court, individuals who now practice Witchcraft in the United States are protected under the Constitution for their beliefs.

Are women more sinful than men? Statistically speaking men hold the title of most sinful, with 93 percent of prisoners being men and 99 percent of rapes committed by men. Thus, to say that women are more sinful goes back to the early biblical descriptions of women such as Lilith and Eve. Their stories were composed by male scholars and thus their sinful images set the false narrative against women into motion.

There have been many misaligned female sinners who struggled under repressive laws, many liberated, and many others sadly lost to history. Let us give validation to all their memories.

Endnotes

1. Pelaia, Ariela. "The Concept of Sin in Judaism." Learn Religions, Aug. 26, 2020, learnreligions.com/do-jews-believe-in-sin-2076758.

2. https://confluence.gallatin.nyu.edu//context/interdisciplinary-seminar/guilt-and-shame-in-oedipus-the-king#

3. https://catholicconvert.com/t-adam-eve-st-abraham-st-moses-did-you-know-some-old-testament-people-are-saints/

4. Seren Bertrand and Azra Bertrand, MD., *Magdallene Mysteries, The Left-Hand Path of the Feminine Christ*, Bear and Company (a division of Inner Traditions), 2020, page 202

5. Seren Bertrand and Azra Bertrand MD., *Magdallene Mysteries, The Left-Hand Path of the Feminine Christ*, Bear and Company (a division of Inner Traditions), 2020, page 165

6. https://www2.kenyon.edu//Depts/Religion/Projects/Reln91/Gender/Gnosticism.htm#

7. https://braidedway.org//rediscovering-sophia-the-goddess-in-christianity/

8. https://christianobserver.net/Sophia-the-divine-feminine-of-gnostics-the-mystery-schools-kabbalah/

9. https://cac.org/ /sophia-wisdom-of-god-2017-11-07/

10. Sophianic Myth | The Fallen Goddess Scenario https://sophianicmth.org

11. Lady Olivia Robertson, *Sophia, Cosmic Consciousness of the Goddess*, FOI Crossroads Media, page 1

12. Lady Haight-Ashton, Pagan Portals: *The Temple Priestesses of Antiquity*, 2022, page 17

13. https://www.ancient-origins.net/news-history-archaeology/tomb-olympias-0015564

14. Muriel Segal, *Painted Ladies*, Stein and Day, first printing 1972, page 12

15. Muriel Segal, *Painted Ladies*, Stein and Day, first printing 1972, page 112.

16. https:/nypost.com/2022/05/26/329-years-later-last-salem-witch-who-wasnt-is-pardoned/

Chapter 2

The Biblical Whores

The seven female prostitutes, whores, and harlots of the bible that I present to you in this chapter all share a common bond. They were mis-labeled as seductive and treacherous women, who were perceived fallen for simply facing life head on with a fervent passion to triumph over the rules of the patriarchy. Their stories are familiar depictions of other fallen women who have also violated orthodox principles and suffered the inevitable punishment that ensued.

These biblical women were wives, Priestesses, Princesses and Queens whose transgressions are well documented by an array of ancient male biblical scholars who distorted their stories to suit their idea of acceptable behavioral and religious teachings. Ironically, the names of these notorious women are far more notable than their male counterparts.

The standard definition of a whore is synonymous with the word prostitute. Usually characterized as a "bad" female, she is a promiscuous woman or courtesan who is involved in numerous sexual encounters. Modern terminology describes her as a sex worker or even a call girl. In ancient times idolatry of false Gods or Goddesses practiced by any women equated to prostitution.

What is the difference between a harlot and a prostitute? The broad definition of a harlot or a tart is a courtesan or a woman who has many sexual encounters. While the definition of a prostitute varies in that the person engages in sexual activity in exchange for payment.

Recounting the many women of mythology who have fallen and been called prostitutes, whores and harlots always brings us back to the bible and its many ancient stories. These are the women of lost legends, considered wicked or depraved. They were women whose stories have morphed into mythological silhouette's. Their legacies reflect the blame and plight of women that has been felt beyond the bible and has sadly continued for thousands of years.

Jezebel

Once such story is that of a Priestess of the Goddess Asherah. Her name was Jezebel and she had her share of ruinous press being portrayed as one of the most scandalous and notorious women of the bible. Even her name brings up visions of immoral desire and erotic overtones. Thus, the name Jezebel seems synonymous with the spirit of sex and the dominance of women's power.

> "Jezebel" has transcended its status as a name and evolved into a word indicating a sexually autonomous woman"[1]

Jezebel is portrayed as an adversary of the prophet Elijah and persecutor of other Jewish prophets. She was a Queen which made her a royal Priestess of the Goddess. It is documented that she encouraged the Israelites in their veneration of Asherah. Honoring the Divine Feminine suddenly became false worship and Jezebel was forced to be the recipient of the vilest press. As the daughter of Ethbaal, the king of Sidon, she married Ahab who she encouraged in the worship of the pagan male God, Baal.

> "Asherah was also identified as the moon goddess who belonged to the family of gods associated with Baal the sun god (Judges 3:7; 6:28). Worship to her included sexual immorality, prostitution, divination, and fortune telling. As a result, the Mosaic Law spoke specifically against Asherah worship (Deuteronomy 16:21)."[2]

Several other women besides Jezebel who appear in biblical text, such as Solomon's wives, also worshipped the Goddess Asherah. Supposedly these wives tried to draw Solomon away from the belief of one true male God!

> "The name Jezebel appears a second time in biblical sources, this time in the Book of Revelation (2:20). Yet another person named Jezebel is accused of falsely calling herself a prophetess while seducing people toward idolatry and fornication."[3]

Some fear the very idea of Jezebel her while others embrace her strength. And she is not the only biblical personage with a dangerous sensual and erotic spirit. One aspect of seductive Lilith's punishment is that she gives birth to dead children each night and her angry spirit endangers other newborns in their cribs. Thus, many who believe such mythological bad press hang a protective amulet near or hanging over each newborns crib. Neither of these famous sensuous biblical women were relegated to Christian sainthood. Perhaps they were too sultry to manage!

Gomer

Another such woman whose tale is told in the Hebrew Bible's Book of Hosea was called Gomer. She was revealed by God to be a prostitute to her husband Hosea, the prophet. It was said that God wanted to put some symbolism into Hosea's life by revealing and accusing his wife! For it was thought in bible text that the love of idols which equates to pagan Gods and Goddesses was likened to the life of a prostitute. Scriptures say that Gomer was also promiscuous and an adulteress. The ancient biblical God seems to liken Gomer's behavior to those who are unfaithful. To worship the Goddess in any form was to the ancient male populations a sin of the most extreme nature provoking character assassinations that many biblical followers still believe today.

> "...because the land is guilty of the vilest adultery in departing from the Lord" (Hosea 1:2)"[4]

Gomer was not a prostitute by profession but simply a promiscuous wife and thus an adulterous woman. Perhaps Gomer was not as sexual as reported but just a Priestess of the Goddess. Thus, her faith was idolatry and for that she was considered a loose or sinful woman. According to the mores of biblical Israel, men were allowed to have sexual access to other women who were not their wives, but woman on the contrary were not allowed any other men besides their husbands.

> "Because of this unequal sexual access to other partners, which itself is based on other gendered asymmetries, ancient Israelite marriage becomes a powerful metaphor, delineating the exclusive boundaries of God's covenant with Israel and Israel's infidelity to that covenant by worshipping other gods."[5]

Gomer had no real biblical voice and thus does not defend herself or explain what her marriage was like to a famous prophet. The Book of Hosea is still read today and considered a valuable sacred text. Ultimately, in the conclusion of this story the one God forgives her act of sin despite himself! What is the moral message here? A fallen woman perhaps not by choice but by necessity to create a cautionary archetype.

Rahab

While Gomer was labeled falsely as a prostitute, Rahab another biblical woman was labeled not only as a young Canaanite prostitute but also a harlot. She appears in 96 bible verses. Like

Jezebel, who was a Priestess of the Mother Goddess Asherah, Rahab, who had a home in Jericho, also venerated Asherah and her God consort, Baal. Both were described in verse as pagan or false idols. There are quite a number of texts that talk about Rahab's home in Jericho, and her connection to Asherah. Perhaps her home was a temple to her Goddess and she was simply a sacred prostitute.

Rahab had a remarkable lineage. She was married to Salmon an Israelite from the tribe of Judah. Her son Boaz married the biblical Ruth. According to scriptures Joseph, the legal father of Jesus was directly descended from Rahab.

Was the lesson of Rahab's story a saga of a worshipper of the Goddess who would certainly become a harlot, as she was referred to in the Book of Joshua. With her lineage she was a candidate to become a penitent heroine for the new faith of one God.

Rahab was touted as a prostitute but she was also a biblical heroine. In the narrative of Joshua 2, and before the conquest of Canaan, two men spies both Israelites were sent by Joshua to view the land of Jericho. The two men came to Rahab's home asking for lodging and information. Though the King demanded that Rahab give up the spies, she defies authority and rescues the Israelites by hiding them on her roof. When the coast was clear she helped them down by rope.

Were the Priestesses Gomer and Rahab, prostitutes, and harlots merely part of the practice of the cult of Sacral Prostitution. Were they Temple Priestesses who performed sex acts ensuring fertility for the soil, prosperity, and safety for their people? Chosen women and men, were considered holy and consecrated to their gods. These biblical stories only represent the sinful aspect or misleading elucidations. The Bible was written from a male perspective with the interpretation of the ethics of a civilization alongside its karmic consequences.

What if these stories of prostitutes and harlots were re-told by members of the female population?

The Whore of Babylon

As we continue our journey, we travel through a millennium of fallen women mythologies to come across the famous Whore of Babylon who makes her appearance in ancient biblical texts. Was she a real person or biblically speaking as many scholars declare simply a symbolic female symbol who impersonated the evil that was within the great city of Babylon. There are references in Revelation describing a woman arrayed in purple and scarlet. She is adorned with gold, jewels and pearls. In her hand she holds a golden cup filled with her sexual and decadent activities. Revelation states that she was the Mystery, and the Mother of Prostitutes and abominations of the Earth.

The city of Babylon falls suddenly in a brutal siege in 539 BCE and reappears years later again within the New Testament. The reference to Babylon can be interpreted as a symbol of the world in rebellion with God's people. The image of the whore becomes the spirit of a seductive society.

In Christendom the term whore is associated with evil and a seven headed beast with ten horns. As mentioned in ancient texts a female whore was synonymous with the guilt of idolatry. But her symbol should be that of a liberated woman as enacted in the Gnostic Mass when she becomes the fertile Mother Earth and the Goddess.

Delilah

Another particularly misunderstood biblical whore was named Delilah and she was definitely one of the most scandalous women in the Bible. She was a Phillistine and lover and then wife to the imposing and long-haired Samson, who threatened to rescue Israel from Phillistine power. The Phillistine Chiefs feared Samson because he held a grudge against them that related to a previous marriage. Thus, the Chiefs desperately needed to find the secret of his power. Though there are slight variations in this ancient biblical tale, the basic premise is that Delilah used her powers of seduction to lure her false husband to lay his head down upon her lap to fall asleep. She then instructed a man to cut off the seven locks of his hair, the source of his strength, thereby striping him of his supremacy and putting him in the control of the Phillistine's. Poor Delilah was probably simply trying to help her people against the deception of her husband. For that she was branded a succubus, whore and prostitute who seduced Samson for eleven hundred silver shekels. As with her sister of the silver screen Cleopatra, Delilah was famously portrayed in numerous Hollywood movies, always playing a voluptuous and treacherous seductress.

The Evangelist Billy Graham saw the gouging of Samson's eyes by the Philistines as his punishment for his lustful desire for Delilah. The ancient Christian scholar Caesarius of Arles viewed Delilah's seduction of Samson as similar to Satan's temptation of Christ. These are extreme examples of misunderstood views that always seem to involve a confident woman who knows her power.

In comparing both Samson's and Adam's fall at the hands of their spouses, we can see a pattern of feminine temptation. Though each was dealt their blows in different settings there are similarities. Both were victims of scandalous acts described in one ancient text after another as being betrayed by their spouses. But more importantly both men became weakened and lost their powers. Ancient texts certainly could not portray either Delilah or Lilith as simply unshackled and assertive women for that would be too dangerous.

Bathsheba
Bathsheba was another such woman who was portrayed as sensuously desirable and ultimately a wicked woman. As the

mother of Solomon, she was married to Uriah the Hittite. But her fame revolves around Solomon's predecessor King David. While walking on his palace roof he saw a very beautiful woman bathing and he lusted after her. He ordered his enquiries to find her and that woman was Bathsheba.

> "she was the daughter of Ammiel (also spelled Eliam); she was impregnated by King David (ca 1010-970 BC) while Uriah was away at war and after Uriah's death (ordered by David), she was taken to wife by David; after the death of the child of their adultery she bore David four sons in Jerusalem".[6]

Was such a lustful action by David acceptable behavior for a King? Because of this scenario, the onus was thrust upon Bathsheba's image and she is unfairly portrayed as a seductress or succubus.

Salome

Though her name was not officially listed in the New Testament it was insinuated that it was the infamous Salome who wanted the head of John the Baptist served on a silver platter. She was a Jewish princess and the daughter of Herod II whose beguiling dance before King Antipas lured him away from salvation and prompted him to adhere to her wishes. Salome becomes another one of the Bible's most luscious and vile seductresses.

Perhaps both Delilah and Salome had a lot in common beyond being sisters of biblical text. Both received pieces of silver for their respective deeds. But what if neither meant for the heinous results to actually happen? What if Delilah merely wanted to weaken Samson? Salome, on the other hand, was influenced by her mother, Herodias, whose dubious gossip claimed that John the Baptist had preached against Heriodias' marriage to Herod

Antipas, her late husband's brother. It was against Jewish Law to marry your brother's wife.

Naively believing her mother, Salome used her wiles to extract revenge.

Salome's famous "Dance of the Seven Veils" portrayed in operas, plays and literature became part of her femme fatale legacy. Famous artists such as Caravaggio, Leonardo DaVinci, and Gustave Moreau are just a sampling of the famous painters that have portrayed both Salome and Delilah in their various seductive guises.

And what of Salome's infamous mother Herodias whose influence of her daughter was very persuasive and who history shows as having the full responsibility for John the Baptist's death.

The fervor of Salome's dance movements certainly rallied the Kings guests into granting her a reward which just happened to be the head of John the Baptist. Certainly, Herodias can be seen historically as an influential, strong-willed, and perhaps a dangerous woman indeed!

Zuleikha

There were many biblical women whose stories are not well known. One such lost woman was given no name in Genesis and simply considered a figure in ancient Jewish texts and Islamic lore, where she was only known as the wife of Potiphar. She had a name and it was Zuleikha, which comes from the Islamic tradition.

Her husband Potiphar, was a Captain of the Pharaoh's guard. Joseph, biblically recognized as one of Jacob's twelve sons, was supposedly falsely accused by Zuleikha of rape and then imprisoned. The wife of Potiphar, of course, was portrayed as the evil seductress. I mention her because she did have a name, Zuleikha, however unimportant and absent it seemed in ancient texts.

Athaliah

There is very little known about the Biblical woman Athaliah, who was supposedly the daughter of King Ahab and Queen Jezebel, though there is nothing recorded about Jezabel being a mother. Some believe Athaliah was really an orphan in the court of the King and possibly the daughter of Omri. Nevertheless, her story is an important one. She was married to Jehoram of Judah who ultimately became the 5th King of Judah. These were turbulent times with assassinations and political changes. After Jehoram's untimely death, Athaliah's son, Ahaziah, became King with Athaliah as Queen Mother. Here is where the story becomes interesting. There is evidence to suggest that Athaliah was possibly a pagan Priestess because she used her power as an "usurper queen" to re-establish the worship of Baal in Judah, the male consort of the Goddess Asherah. In this period of upheaval Athaliah became involved in stopping a rebellion, was captured, and executed. Here we have another biblical woman who was considered sinful in her opinionated and strong behavior. Thus, the biblical lesson was to remind women to stay unobserved and silent, and definitely not venerate false idols.

The Sisters Oholah and Oholibah

Another story of false idols is described in Chapter 23 of the Book of Ezekiel where there is a profound reference to Oholah and her sister Oholibah who engaged in spiritual prostitution or spiritual infidelity in their youth. Not really flesh and blood women, their stories border on the side of a mythological religious principle. They are thought to be only symbolic names for the Kingdom of Israel, ten tribes in the north and the Kingdom of Judah or Jerusalem, two tribes to the south. Ezekiel describes spiritual infidelity between Israel and Jerusalem or Judah as if they were indeed two sisters.

"In Ezekiel's allegory; she was the girl who stood for Samaria, capital of the Northern Kingdom of Israel; with her younger sister Oholibah standing for Jerusalem"[7]

Ezekiel chose these names with purpose. Oholah is defined as "her own tent or tabernacle, whereas Oholibah means "my tabernacle is in her." Jerusalem is where it was thought God established the Israelite religion, so Oholah representing Samaria or Israel was a separate place of worship apart from the center Jerusalem, of her younger sister Oholibah They were also daughters of the same mother because Israel and Judah were originally one nation, Israel. Ezekiel describes Oholah as playing the harlot with the false idols of the Assyrians, who eventually conquered Israel. Deporting her people to Assyria, was Ezekiel's explanation of God's punishment on Israel.

Ezekiel then portrays Oholibah as even more evil and sexual than her older sister. As a prostitute she commits the ultimate sign of idolatry with the Babylonian idols. And so, the story goes that God also reaps his punishment on Jerusalem by allowing the Babylonians to capture the people of Jerusalem. God has alienated himself from both tribes. The lesson is that God can be jealous and his anger knows no bounds if worship of idols persists.

How appropriate for the time to use the names and characters of two women described as whores to explain away religious issues confronted by two tribes.

Tamar

Finally, we have the story Tamar who appears in Genesis and was described as a wife, mother, and widow. She was widowed to both Er and Onan and both were arranged marriages. Women had very little say in their futures. It was through fear of losing her one son that she disguised herself as a harlot or prostitute in order to become pregnant by her father-in-law Judah. She then bore him twin sons, Perez, and Zorah. It was said that with the birth of these twin sons and subsequently their sons, Tamar becomes the ancestor of Joseph, husband of Mary, Mother of Jesus. Tamar joins her other biblical sisters in the age-old critique of being misunderstood to issue a stern example in male supremacy. It seems that any woman, no matter their lineage, who dared to know her own mind must have been a whore! Is the Bible guilty of historical distortions regarding its portrayal of women? How can we ever find the whole truth without first understanding all aspects of the past. Herstory views inaccuracies in a different light from accepted history. The fact that many biblical women were debased and viewed as scandalous, insured that they definitely made their mark in reality and mythology. Though many had their stories buried within sermonized pages others became romanticized figures of art and literature. The more we say their names and tell their stories the more power we give to their fascinating memories.

Endnotes

1. https://occult-world.com/jezebel/
2. https://www.compellingtruth.org/asherah.html#
3. https://occult-world.com/jezebel/
4. https://www.crosswalk.com/faith/women/gomer-an-unfaithful-woman-with-a-powerful-message.html
5. https://jwa.org//encyclopedia/article/gomer-bible
6. M.L. Mastro, *All the Women of the Bible*, Castle Books, 2004 page 33
7. M.L. Mastro, *All the Women of the Bible*, Castle Books, 2004 page 97

Chapter 3

The Saints

How does one really define the term "saint"? One meaning is that it is a virtuous person of exceptional holiness, who will surely go to a heavenly reward after death. Scriptural definitions vary immensely. Saints in scriptures are not just holy but particularly designated as God's special people. Saints are revered, prayed to, and often venerated by many who believe in the Roman Catholic and Orthodox Christian doctrines.

There are many women in the annals of folklore and history, though thought of in the derogatory, who did not start out as sinners, but eventually traveled the road to sainthood. Many were venerated mystical personas, who as Goddesses were ancient cultural and spiritual icons. Their holy images could not be thwarted or erased by any new wave of religious thinking that creep though the early centuries. This meant that their importance to the populace of ancient civilizations could not be shunned. Instead, their personas very systemically morphed into the new and more acceptable saintly images of Christendom. Organized Christian religions might have changed the image of these familiar Divine sources that empowered and gave humanity comfort for a millennium, but they did not disappear. With this ancient universal transposition, a sort of transfer of power, the different yet similar names still housed the same Divine message.

Melissa

There are many stories of Goddesses who became saints. In ancient Greece a Priestess was called a "Melissa." Melissa means bee and their symbolism in many cultures was the life-giving quality of the Goddess, for she creates the honey which many ancients considered to be the Nectar of the Gods. How appropriate that this Goddess quality morphed into Saint Melissa who mythology says drove off a barbarian horde from her nunnery by using her power to turn itching bees against them.

Brigit

The Goddess Brigit is a well-known and important example of a pagan Divinity who morphed into a Catholic Saint. Brigit, Brid, Brigid, or Bridget in Celtic religion was an ancient Goddess of the arts, poetry and smithcraft. In her triple or trinity aspect she also represents healing and divination. Brigit was originally thought to be a Sun Goddess because she was born at sunrise, thus her connection to the sacred flame.

"A tower of flame burst forth from her forehead from Earth to Heaven."[1]

She was the daughter of the Druid God, Dagda, from the Tuatha De' Danann of Ireland. As the keeper of the cauldron, she was in charge of the elemental water, as well as fire. In her shrine at Kildare there was a perpetual flame tended by nineteen virgin priestesses called Daughters of the Flame. With the onset of the Catholic religion in Ireland, the shrine became the first convent and her Priestesses morphed, somewhat forcibly into becoming nuns. The ancient traditions adapted into the new spiritual thoughts and her ancient pagan holy day of Imbolc became Candlemas in the Christian Churches. Today there are one hundred holy wells dedicated to the Christian Saint Brigit in Ireland.

The Goddess Brigit was never a sinner, she was transformed into a Saint to ensure that the new religious creed was accepted. She fell from Goddess to Saint so her worshipers could remain strong and loyal. Now the powerfully loved Goddess Brigit lives on in the guise of an equally loved Saint.

Saint Brigit's feast day is on February 1st in the Roman Catholic, Eastern Orthodox and Anglican Churches. The ancient Pagan festival of Imbolc and Candlemas of the sacred flame, coincide thus linking Saint and Goddess feast days.

Barbara

The story of Saint Barbara from the third century is uniquely different from her any of her counterparts. She was proclaimed a sinner. Her sin, amongst her people, was that she left the ancient pagan religion to convert to Christianity. Beheaded by her pagan father in retaliation for her conversion, she became a Christian martyr and ultimately a Saint. In punishment for this horrid action, her father was struck by lightning and killed as he walked home. So, once again, the definition of a sinner shifts and changes according to the scruples of the religious community and the social mores. Her story takes her from sinner to Saint and then shifts from Goddess to Saint. In parts of both the Georgian and Mesopotamian mythologies, the Goddess Barbale was the Goddess of the Sun and fertility ensuring good harvests and healthy livestock for her people. As Christianity came to Georgia the Goddess Barbale morphed into Saint Barbara within the Georgian Orthodox Christian Church. Though a Christian Saint her feasts still have pagan origins and traditions. It is said that in the mountainous regions of Georgia, pagan rituals in her honor sometimes eclipse the Christian.

Olga

Saint Olga, a venerated Saint in the Eastern Orthodox Christian church started life as the wife of Prince Igor 1 of Kievan, whom she married in 903 CE. Prince Igor was assassinated by the Drevlians, a neighboring tribe. Olga was branded as a murderous sinner who took revenge upon her husband's killers by massacring everyone responsible. Olga subsequently ruled as regent on behalf of Igor's son, Syiatoslay, with the support of the army and her people. She was the first women to rule Kievan. History downplays the importance of her rule and focuses on the bloody revenge attributed to her. She was really a good ruler who was responsible for changes in legal reform, the first in Eastern Europe.

Then Olga according to possibly bias historical reports, suddenly had an epiphany while visiting Constantinople and converted to Christianity. She was baptized in 957 CE taking the name Elena. She believed her calling was to repent and travel as a missionary. She worked tirelessly converting anyone who would listen about Christianity. She died in 969 CE. Once again, a so-called sinner becomes a Saint! Was Olga really that horrid or did the historical accounts exaggerate her actions? History is an interpretation of an event in the past, and all too often an inaccurate one.

Mary of Egypt

Another so-called sinner turned into a Saint was St. Mary of Egypt, born in 344 CE and died in 421 CE. She was originally known as Maria Aegyptiaca when she began her early life as a seductress in the great and ancient city of Alexandria. Theologians and historians reveal that she was drawn to a life of debauchery by her need to dominate men rather than for any financial rewards. Here we have another fallen woman, and one clearly pictured as a succubus. I believe she was falsely portrayed as an uncontrollable seductress without morals or conscience. There seems to be a common historical theme with sexually free women being mis-judged and branded as sinners. Considered a depraved individual, as with most similar stories Mary repents. The historical version of her story describes her boarding a ship sailing for the Holy City of Jerusalem, where she repents of her passionate sins. It is in the Holy City that she has a cathartic moment and renews her faith in the Church. She then spends the rest of her life in the desert as a hermit fighting her depraved temptations.

I have not been able to locate the exact date when she was made a Saint but her feast day is April 1st and she is honored in both the Roman Catholic and Orthodox churches.

"She is the patroness of chastity, temptations of the flesh, and skin diseases."[2]

Most of what little is known about Mary is found in the *Vita* a Latin biography that was written by St. Sophronius who lived from 560 to 638 CE. St. Sophronius received the information from oral tradition.

Though forgiven, Mary did begin her life as an accused succubus. This is a term used to describe too many of our fallen women, A succubus is a female entity who appears in dreams to seduce men, through mesmerizing and erotic sexual activity. In romantic art and sculpture, she is often depicted as a beautiful seductress or enchantress. The word itself comes from the Latin succubae or paramour. A succubus is also a supernatural earth wanderer who seeks out her victims in sensual play. And of course, though many ancient women have been defined as having a succubus nature, the most famous one, of course was Lilith. Goddess to some and demon to others.

Pelagia

Pelagia was a 5th century woman, who led a very interesting life. She was thought to be a sexually adventurous women who intoxicated her lovers. Fitting the category of a "painted lady" she was an actress of Antioch and a stage performer who sold herself for pearls and jewels that she famously draped around her neck and body. She wore such gossamer clothing that an onlooker would surely behold the outline of her body. Transfixed and delighted, her lovers gave up everything in their lives, family, and money for her. Not wanting to give credit to her beauty, some accounts suggested that she actually drugged her lovers, but nothing was ever proven.

Nonetheless she was another consummate succubus. In the midst of everything happening in her life, she heard a bishop's sermon. It not only mesmerized her but thrust her into viewing herself as a sinful woman and a servant of the devil. She was so inspired that she suddenly converted to Christianity. Was the sermon so very life changing and all consuming? Obviously, because she became a Nun, spending the rest of her life in solitude and prayer. Her transition from a fallen women to one of devotion to the Christian God was rewarded with her becoming Saint Pelagia also known as Pelagia the Penitent and to never forget her past, Pelagia the Harlot.

Was Pelagia in her early years really such a bad woman? Perhaps her saga was like many other stories of women of substance who held the power of attraction and were punished by society only to be rewarded when they adhered to the current rules of conviction. In none of the stories of fallen women do we hear about the shared responsibility of men. It was her male lovers, of their free will, who showered Pelagia with gifts and attention. One must wonder why a woman of such success would suddenly turn so drastically to doubting the validity of her life? Is it possible that her history was reinterpreted and written in a way to show a harsh lesson for wayward women? A culture's definition of sinfulness must evolve into remorse in order to find the reward of redemption. In other words, stay the recognized course.

Angela of Foligno

Another typical yet intriguing story of a Saint is that of Angela of Foligno who was born in 1248 CE and died in 1309 CE. She was recently canonized by Pope Francis. Her reputation was not very flattering because she was described as a vain and materialistic woman who valued possessions and pleasure more than her family life. Angela was born to a wealthy Italian family and thus married a wealthy man of high social standing. It has been documented, perhaps with bias, that she had several children but cared only for wealth and status. She was also accused of adultery, though no actual proof has been found.

Suddenly at the age of 40 she had an epiphany and converted to Christianity, realizing how pointless and superficial her life had become. Tragically, within three years of her conversion her mother, husband, and children all died. This prompted Angela to sell all her worldly possessions and join a secular Franciscan order. She also founded a female religious group to serve the poor. Angela recorded the history of her conversion in her *Book of Visions and Instructions*. It usually takes two to or three miracles for one to be qualified to be venerated and canonized as a Saint. Angela seemed to bypass these qualifications and was canonized because of her spiritual writing and her religious community, which is still active today. The Catholic Church declared Angela to be a Saint in 2013. Once again, we have a story of bad press and redemption within the context of accepted norms.

Priscilla

From fallen to forgotten the stories of ancient women are being slowly uncovered and their value reappraised and finally appreciated. One such important story to re-discover is that of Priscilla, a Roman woman of Jewish heritage from the 1st century. She was a teacher and possibly the first example of a female Christian preacher. Along with her husband, Aquila, they became two of the earliest Christian missionaries. As a friend and co-worker of the Apostle Paul, Priscilla was not thought of as a Goddess, nor was she a sinner. I mention her merely to emphasize a fact about forgotten women in ancient historical and biblical texts. She is always mentioned alongside her husband as if she could not stand alone. As a couple they are mentioned together in the New Testament but never separately. They were even canonized as Saints together in the Catholic, Greek Orthodox and Antiochian Orthodox Churches. But a few brave scholars believe that she might have been the sole author of the Book of Hebrews, though her name was omitted from authorship. Though rarely documented, women of that time did teach men. The engrained belief that woman was made from man created a reality whereby women were not given fair recognition for scholarly or independent pursuits.

Louise de La Valliere

Louise de La Valliere was born in the provincial town of Tours, France on August 6, 1644. As fate would decree, she would ultimately become Louis XIV's favorite mistress from 1661 until 1667. It was the maneuvering and intrigues of her family and friends in and around the court at Versailles that brought Louise to the King's attention. Brought up in a devote Catholic family Louise was fortunate in her religious training. It was this training that would serve her well in later years. At fourteen Louise was pretty, blond, and modest, with a character of good sense and prudence. A highly romantic girl, Louise rivaled in praise and attention.

> "Quite naturally Louise was extremely pleased with this public praise and with the sense of superiority it gave her. Years later she was to reproach herself severely for this most human reaction."[3]

Many of her biographers claim that even at young age she wanted to enter the religious life, but there is no evidence to support this assertion.

During her years at court Louise's life was filled with parties always wearing the Kings presents with jewels on her arms, in her ears and around her neck. Content in the moment Louise reveled in her glory. But deep inside her soul, probably because of her religious upbringing, she would oftentimes dwell upon the words of the Court's preacher, the Jesuit Louis Bourdaloue. He most likely directed them at her when he preached about the woman Mary Magdalane, whom he declared to be a sinner and who dried her Lords feet with her hair.

Louise was aware of the temptations around her and yet she was full of joy in the hope of eventual forgiveness. After nine years of life in Court where she let her undisciplined emotions and tangled passions govern her life she began to change. She dressed more demurely and attended the Catholic Mass daily, frequently in the Nun's chapel.

"As she listened to the priest's word and the nuns chanting, peace came to her very soul. Over and over again that liturgy spoke of God's mercy to sinful men"[4]

It was only a short time later when Louise de la Valliere asked to leave the court and walked into the entrance of the Carmel Convent at Saint Jaques. It was in 1604 that the first Carmelite Nuns came to France. Louise had stayed in one such convent as a young girl before going to the Court of Louis XIV. In 1673 Louise was accepted into the Carmel at the age of 30 and for the next 36 years she practiced penance for her sins. Obscure and forgotten, her life was full of passion for Court life and then abruptly for the life within a Carmel Monastery. Odd considering her transformation, Louise was not given sainthood though she was considered very saintly!

Catholic Carmelite Nuns are totally cloistered, almost like hermits behind the walls of their monasteries. They see no one upon entering except for their fellow Nuns. It is a very simple contemplative and meditative way of life where they are devoted to living in the infinite space of constant prayer. They do not mingle with the outside world.

I have visited the convent in New Jersey and spoken to Mother Mary Joseph, the author of *The King's Favorite the Life of Louise De la Valliere* on numerous occasions. An amazing woman of great depth, she should not be forgotten.

Saintly Goddesses were the original influencers. Their characteristics strayed from the idea of divinity to that of a more human guise. In their personas of purity and goodness saintly humans are venerated and prayed to just as their divine Goddess predecessors were. Still in Christianity there is only one divine source. The Council of Christendom Bishops representing the Church in the Bithynian city of Nicaea, now Turkey was organized by the Roman Emperor Constantine I in 325 CE. The Council made papal decisions and proclamations that designated the choice of gospels and beliefs that have since become the foundation of the Christian world. It was around this time in history that Goddesses began to lose their influence which paved the way for the Christian world's acceptance of only one God or Divine source. Perhaps purely coincidental but the idea of the Sacred Feminine suddenly fell.

Endnotes

1. https://www.sacredwicca.com/brigit
2. https://aleteia.org//2017/10/31/st-mary-of-egypt-from-a-life-of-sin-to-sainthood/
3. Mother Mary Joseph, O.C.D. *The King's Favorite the Life of Louise De la Valliere,*. Carmelite Monastery, Flemington, NJ published with Ecclesiastical permission by The Queen's Press, Carmel of Maria Regina, 87609 Green Hill Road, Eugene, Oregon 07401 Chapter II page 11
4. Mothe Mary Joseph, O.C.D., *The King's Favorite the Life of Louise De la Valliere*, Carmelite Monastery, Flemington, NJ published with Ecclesiastical permission by The Queen's Press, Carmel of Maria Regina, 87609 Green Hill Road, Eugene, Oregon 07401 Chapter VIII page 60

Chapter 4

The Goddesses

Part I: Unearthed

According to archeologists, historians and scholars, worship of the Divine Feminine in the form of fertility images began around the Paleolithic period, 2.5 million years ago to 10,000 BCE, which is thought to be humanity's longest recorded period on Earth. Discoveries unearthed from the Neolithic period, approximately 9,500 to 8000 BCE, brought forth an abundance of small mis-identified female figurines. These crude statues were for many years never acknowledged as Goddesses, but simply thought to be ritual offerings to insure not only fertility but general abundance.

History records a shift in the dynamics and power of the Goddess as societies matured and evolved. Her validity and position faded though the millennium amidst one religious and cultural war after another. The status of matriarchal societies fell way below that of the new ruling patriarchal view. Because these unearthed figures were thought to have little or no value other than as offerings, the power and status of the Goddess was relegated to ancient lore.

Then on August 7, 1908 a workman named Johann Veran near a village in Lower Austria unearthed what is now known to be the earliest image of a feminine figure dating more than 25,000 years ago. The excavation was conducted by archeologists Josef Szombathy and Hugo Obermaier.

This tiny figure of approximately four inches was carved from limestone and tinted in red ochre and stimulated a profusion of excited interest amongst scholars. She portrayed a female image unlike any classical Roman or Egyptian version of a Goddess previously discovered. She could only be described as a nude woman with abundantly large breasts and fully extended belly. Now housed in the Natural History Museum in Vienna Austria, she is our first known Goddess image and an earthy Mother to be sure!

Traveling to ancient Mesopotamia into Egypt and then Rome and Greece, we suddenly see modern archeological discoveries of recognized Goddess figures stately and imposing, that are not considered fertility figurines. With the accumulation of centuries of archeological facts now available, scholars confirm that Goddesses held court in ancient temple complexes and were not only worshipped by their cults of Priestesses but by the populace. These were deities of great and powerful importance. Athena, the patron Goddess of ancient Athens was honored and worshipped for the power and prestige she bestowed upon Athens. In ancient Rome the Vestal Virgin Priestesses who honored the Goddess Vesta keep the sacred hearth and flame burning in her name. The flame was the symbolic power of Rome. The worship and influence of the Greek Goddess Cybele traveled as far as the Roman Empire, where her power protected the Roman state.

With new discoveries and ancient accounts unearthed daily, the re-birth of the Goddess is rising. Instead of continuing her descent into extinction she is making a vibrant and profound comeback. History is becoming herstory.

"At the dawn of Western civilization, 25,000 years of 'herstory' of the Goddess' bountiful creativity were obliterated."
—Lynn Rogers, *Edgar Cayce and the Eternal Feminine*[1]

Part II: Dark and Light

Regretfully, humanity has a universal propensity to fear the unknown. The Feminine Divine was and still is an enigma to many. Goddesses of light such as Demeter and Gaia reflect the personas of life through motherhood, fertility, and the richness of the harvest. Their qualities do not arise from fear, for they are thought to be standing in the sunshine under the light of the sun and moon. However, there are other Goddesses who share a darker trait. We find them in the forms of Kali, Lilith, Nyx and Nephthys to name a few. They embody qualities of chaos, sexual freedom, mystery, and the transformation from death to re-birth. They are known as the Dark Goddesses who can be considered fallen simply because they are a paradox. One metaphor for darkness is shadow and for light purity. Though deities are wrongly labelled with one or the other characteristic, Goddesses in herstory encompass both. Honoring the dark aspect within a Goddess is not for the faint hearted. Her Crone wisdom is not something that can be wrapped and tied with a bow. If we seek her insight, she will awaken and challenge us to be inquisitive and embrace her mystifying archetype that resides within us. The maiden or mother aspect of Goddesses offers one view of deity, whereas insight into the darker side of Goddesses offers the other side of re-birth that begins with transformation.

Did the Dark Goddesses of mythology become conveniently incorporated into the myth of the fallen women because they are so fearsome, deeply mystifying or simply a threat to authority? Many Goddesses fit the archetype of the wise old Crone. They are the mysterious practitioners of Witchcraft. As much healers as mediators between death and rebirth, they represent the secrets of life and the dark unknown. They have challenging characteristics and thus became labeled as Dark Goddesses. Psychics. oracles and sibyls channel the darker Goddesses whose mystical vibrations encourage a deeper grasp of the unexplained and the meditative state that brings awareness of the beyond.

There are thousands of Goddesses and as one who acknowledges many, I only channel and honor a few.

Isis and Mary

There is one universally known Goddess who is multi-faceted and encompasses both light and dark characteristics. She was never truly forgotten nor did she transition into sainthood. Her lasting persona has morphed into one of the most revered Saints in all of Christendom. The Goddess is Isis and the Saint is St Mary, the Blessed Virgin. Isis, the Egyptian Goddess of ten-thousand names is also a Moon and radiant Solar Goddess. She is the Lady of Rebirth and to the ancient Egyptians she was also a model wife and mother. Her many guises were thought to be a link between the Deities and royalty. Pyramid texts record that the ruling Pharoah's drank from her breasts the divine milk. She was the Pharoah's symbolic mother. Her maternal image was compared to the Greek Goddess Gaia and the Roman Goddess Demeter plus many other ancient Deities that rule over fertility, harvest, and grain. It has been said that until WWII there were still functioning Temples in her honor.

Worship of the Goddess Isis spread from Egypt and into the entire ancient Greco-Roman world. It was her devoted Priestesses who turned her worship into one of the largest spiritual cults. Her persona under Christianity could not disappear. Most importantly Isis inspired sacred reverence in her similarity to St. Mary and both divinities shared special cults of veneration.

She was transformed beyond that of a mother to morph into the personas of numerous worldly Goddesses including: Aset, Aust, Eenohebis, Sekhmet, Hathor, Persephone, Tethys, and Athena to name a few.

Saint Mary also had many names: St. Mary the Virgin, The Blessed Virgin Mary, Mary Mother of God or simply the Virgin Mary. Mary is thought to be the spiritual mother of humanity and the greatest Christian saint.

The story of the revered Goddess Isis is as complex as her marriage to her love match, the great God Osiris. In Egypt order and balance were very important and Osiris represented both. While his brother Set was associated with violence and chaos. Set was the vengeful and jealous brother who killed Osiris. Though there are many versions to this story, one is that the jealously came from a supposed sexual act between Osiris and Nephthys, Set's wife. Here we have a struggle between order and disorder and the interruption of life by death. In some versions Set disguises himself as a wild animal to slay Osiris while others imply that Osiris's was drowned. Nonetheless Set dismembers Osiris's body and scatters the pieces throughout Egypt.

With the aid of her sister Nephthys, Isis searches everywhere for her beloved husband Osiris. But she also has help from the Egyptian God Thoth who has magical and healing powers and the God Anubis who rules over embalming and funerary rites. Aware that he has been dismembered Isis and Nephthys gather all of Osiris' body parts in order to fully restore his body. A story of resurrection and rebirth, so similar to the Christian story.

Once Osiris is momentary made whole, Isis quickly copulates with him to conceive their son and rightful heir, Horus. Some ancient texts say Isis took on the image of a hovering falcon with wings outstretched during the copulation, reminiscent of the wings of the Angel who came to Mary of the immaculate conception. The Coffin Texts, which are said to be the missing link between the Pyramid Texts and the Book of the Dead, mentions a vague spell that the copulation and impregnation was actually a bolt of lightning.

Mary's story involves the Angel Gabriel surrounded in light, whose visitation announced that Mary would conceive a child, without ever knowing a man. This was an immaculate conception, with the child being the son of God. Isis in her dark aspect had some power over death. She conceived a child while copulating with her deceased husband and taking unto her his sperm in order to carry Horus who was the son of the God Osiris. Was this another sort of immaculate conception revisited?

Isis was never made a Saint. She continues to be a Goddess most sanctified throughout many cultures. But St. Mary the mother of Jesus was a Saint. And here lies the transformation. Isis becomes the forerunner to the Blessed Virgin Mary in Catholic and St. Mary in Christian myths.

The enormous array of statutes, drawings and carvings of Isis show her seated on a throne, suckling the young Horus who sits on her lap. Saint Mary mimics this image of Isis holding the child in her arms with her own child Jesus. Both Isis and Mary were vital links between the Divine and in Isis' case royalty and Mary's humanity.

Two spiritual Mothers who gave birth to sons of Gods. Isis crowned with stars and Mary crowned with a sparkling halo. Both have a devoted cult of Priestesses and Temples; Churches and faithful followers.

But the influential story of St. Mary, Queen of Heaven continues. In image after image, she wears a sky-blue gown decorated with stars with her foot carefully placed upon a crescent moon. She also has a halo or crown of stars upon her head which is reminiscent of the Goddesses Ishtar, the Babylonian Goddess of Love and the Sumerian Goddess of sex and power, Inanna. All these Goddesses have similar symbolizations and all were often depicted wearing glorious crowns. Many other images show Mary stepping upon a coiled serpent representing the Goddess Lilith. Lilith is the serpent who tempted Eve in the Garden of Eden. Is the Christian icon Mary crushing any remembrance of Lilith's power?

There are many more Goddesses of Antiquity who have morphed into the image of Isis or St. Mary. Two of the Norse Goddesses Frigg and Freya are associated with wisdom, fertility, and love. And both were ultimately replaced with a single holiness in the name of the Virgin Mary, during the course in the rise of Christianity. To make the historical mythologies more complicated the Goddess Feya is sometimes associated with the Germanic St. Ursula. Within the myths relating to Ursula's story one can surmise that she probably became a saint because as a Christian she refused to marry any of her Pagan suitors. Ursula's story fits into a biblical pattern of virginal woman becoming saintly. Was this and is it still a message to women that purity, like St. Mary, the Virgin Mother, is really something to reward? For ancient women the message was clear. The humbleness of purity was one choice balanced by the choice of loving motherhood. There was no place for independence or sexuality, thus the image of the fallen women suffered greatly at the hands of historians and theologians.

Here we have a clear representation of the descent of the Goddess Isis who morphed and rose into the image of St Mary with many other Goddesses following suit though the ages. To rise is to survive. The Goddess thrives within herstory.

Ereshkigal and Inanna

Ereshkigal is the Sumerian Queen of the Dead. As ruler of the underworld, she summons the dead to her. She is the older sister of the well-known Goddess Inanna, whose descent into the underworld to seek self-fulfillment and rebirth is well documented in ancient prose. Inanna travels into the underworld and passes through seven gates and at each removes one piece of clothing until she finally stands naked and pure before the throne of her sister Ereshkigal. She has transformed. We see many images that portray Ereshkigal, as a lion-headed woman who suckles her cubs, to a winged creature standing on the back of two lions. She is sometimes also flanked by owls, similar to depictions of the Goddess Lilith. Inanna and Ereshkigal are perfect representations of the light, and dark aspects of the Goddess. Ereshkigal can become an excellent guide and teacher as you traverse the shadows of your own life.

Let us lift the Goddesses complex archetype from the darkness and welcome her rise not her descent. Celebrate the divine dance of the universe with her and rejoice to witness her ascension into the light of common consciousness. She is no longer fallen or forgotten.

Egyptian Goddesses of Life and Death

The spiritual beliefs of many ancient cultures and their societies centered around an array of Goddesses and Gods. These are powerful entities that the ancients believed must be honored and appeased, in order to keep the safety and abundance of their people in balance. Ancient Egyptians honored hundreds of Goddesses and Gods but as a patriarchal society they placed their trust in the Sun God Ra and his cultural counterparts Ptah and Amun. The Egyptian pantheons helped one in life, but their main role was to guide one through the dark and challenging labyrinthine afterworld.

As we travel through these ancient mythologies, we encounter countless matriarchal forms from the Mother Goddess personas of creation to the heroic Warrior Goddesses who protected ancient cities. Statues, cave drawings, images on pottery and tablets, all show powerful images that influenced changing Egyptian religious teachings for a millennium.

There are several well-known Mother Goddesses within the Egyptian pantheon who stand in the light and did not entirely fall from view. Much credit can be given to the discoveries of coffin and pyramid texts that have kept these names in the eyes and minds of scholars very much alive. One such deity is the Mother Goddess Mut, a primal deity who is associated with the primordial waters of Nu from which everything was birthed. And with every spiritual civilization within the bright dawn of creation, there is a balance of darker energy.

Which brings us to Ammit, one of the Egyptian Goddesses of the Underworld. She devours the hearts of those who led evil lives on earth. Kauket whose symbol is the snake is known as the Goddess of Darkness and Kebechet who also shares the snake symbol is the Goddess of embalming liquid and purification. Ancient societies marveled at the mystery of the snake in its shedding skin and continuous rebirth. Comfortable in the cold darkness of the earth, the snake or serpent has always been a symbol of the unknown and oftentimes associated with a Dark Goddess or a fallen woman. The phrase she is like a snake is not considered to be flattering!

These mystifying Goddesses appear throughout history and herstory. They test our abilities to embrace the mysteries that encompass the profound questions of life and death. Our very souls are laid bare in conjecture. Are Dark Goddesses really just those who test our perception of life, death, and the concept of eternity? Thus, can we interpret that in being associated with the dark makes them fallen? It is easy to categorize those who do not fit within the safety of innocence as not only different but descended from the norm. The common interpretation of a Dark Goddess is also one of trepidation or even dread.

Another Goddess from the Egyptian pantheon is the fearsome Egyptian Goddess Wadjet who was depicted as a cobra, oftentimes coiled upon the head of the God Ra. She was his protector and thus the protector of all the royal Pharaohs. Her power as such was in the *Eye of Wadjet* called the Uraeus symbol, consisting of an image of a sun disk with a rearing cobra. Also, this image had a connection to the symbol of the eye of Ra. But Wadjet in her protective nature had a dark side:

"She's known as *The Lady of Devouring Flame,* who uses her fire to destroy her enemies, just like a serpent would use its venom."[2]

Then we have Neith, an Egyptian Goddess of creation but also of war and hunting whose symbol was two crossed arrows over a shield. Once again where there is dark, there is always light.

"She is said to make the weapons of warriors and to guard their bodies when they died."[3]

Kali

The compelling image of the Hindu Goddess Kali has the reputation as a destroyer of demons and she is the black one in Sanskrit. Her frightening image depicts her with four undulating arms and legs. With her right hands she holds out blessings and with her left a severed head and a bloody sword which represents the burden of ignorance and ego. In the beginning there was only darkness and she represents that darkness from which everything was created. She is black as the darkest night. She is also the Goddess of preservation and nature. Her long black flowing hair represents freedom. At times she also transitions into a Mother Goddess with a nurturing and yet devouring aspect. In the Hindu tantric tradition, she is a loving primordial Mother Goddess where she is referred to as Kali Ma. Thus, with dark there is light. Though represented as dark there is light in her hidden aspects that appear to many and add to her powerful mystic. She is still defined as a frightening Dark Goddess.

The complexities of interpretation when trying to define the descent of the Goddess, or one that some consider fallen such as Kali, perplexes the mind and becomes a spiritual conundrum. There is a school of somewhat dubious scholarly thought that defines certain Goddesses as really fallen angels or the other way around. Is that why we consider those who challenge our perceptions of the mysterious dark? Does dark really mean evil? Clearly no, for in defining some of the great Goddesses of our ancient world it simply means that they hold not only the light nurturing warmth of the mother, but they continuously challenge our perception of what lies beyond life, the infinite. Through the millennium, and even to the present day, what humanity cannot define becomes troubling and with this confusion comes mis-judgement and misinterpretation. The mythological fallen Goddesses evolutionary cycle descended into a perplexed consciousness that distorted what is considered the theoretical female norm.

Apate and Eris

The ancient Greek Goddess, Apate, had an impressive lineage as the daughter of the God of Darkness, Erebos, and Nyx, the Goddess of Night. A true Dark Goddess from birth, she represented deceit and deception and was known to be cruel. She certainly was dark and a Goddess that could be defined as fallen. Why did our ancestors even acknowledge a fearsome Goddess? My interpretation is that she was the frightening counterpart to the warrior Gods, who needed to be appeased in order to ensure the safety of the social order.

Another Dark Goddess was the Greek Eris whose twin brother was Ares, the God of War. As a warrior she is portrayed, perhaps unfairly, as loving conflict and discord. Mythology tells us that Eris was scorned by the other Greek Gods and in that regard could be defined as descending from the light and plunging into darkness.

Artemis

The Greek Queen Artemisia I was the ruler of the city of Halicarnassus. She was born in that city around 520 BCE, near what is now Bodrum, Turkey. She was a warrior queen who began her rule upon the death of her husband, whose name has been lost to history. Ancient playwrights such as Aristophanes described her as a strong and haughty warrior woman. Historians compared her to the female Amazons believed to be an ancient culture of female warriors in Greek mythology who were fearless and skillful fighters. Herodotus the ancient Greek historian and geographer best known for writing the history of the Greco-Persian Wars writes that she was actually a naval commander in that war. Xerxes the Great, the Persian King who ruled the ancient Achaemenid Empire, selected Artemisia to be the only female among his male commanders. As a naval officer she commanded five ships that had a reputation for fierceness and heroism. Sadly, she did fall from grace when she was described as a cowardly pirate! Among her accomplishments beyond her successes at sea she built a mausoleum that was known as one of the seven wonders of the ancient world. The contradictions about her history might never sort out, but she was a powerful mortal woman who mythology morphed into a Goddess. As Artemis, the twin sister of the God Apollo, she was the Wild Goddess of the Hunt who surrounded herself with both nymphs and hunters. In one image after another Artemisia's Goddess persona is seen holding a bow and arrow alongside a stag. The many aspects of the mortal Artemisia's ancient tale simply show that women were strong warriors which reflects in her morphed persona as the Goddess Artemis and her compliment the Roman Goddess Diana. A powerful woman can rise to a mythological status.

Hecate

The Greek Goddess Hecate guards the crossroads with a warrior's strength, holding a torch in one hand and frightening barking dogs flanking her side. She is also depicted as holding a key and snakes. As one of the many protectors of Athens she has a triple aspect that encompasses the totality of the maiden, mother, and crone. As the wise old crone, she assists us in our search to discover our true pathway in this life, by using her key to open the door that will allay our fears. The picture she represents can be a deterrent to many who fear to venture forward and would rather live a life of common predictability.

Those who wish to awaken all the unique possibilities within do not see her an old hag but as a young and lovely wispy maiden who simply shows us the way.

Vesta and the Vestal Virgins of Rome

The common goal in ancient societies and even today in our modern world has always been for one more powerful sect to achieve dominance over another. Regretfully, there cannot be a winner without a loser. Losing balance creates distress. Power is vital in any society and when that is challenged there is usually censure which leads to accusation. Throughout the ancient world women have at times been considered worrisome and too uncontrollable. The powerful female Priestess Oracles of the ancient world held court in many societies with their visions and prophecies. They tipped the balance of power which resulted in many fallen Priestesses. For example, the Vestal Virgins of Rome who honored the Goddess Vesta, were held to a strict code of behavior and even a slight transgression was punishable by various degrees of castigation. The Goddess Vesta was immensely revered and considered on the lighter side of divinity. Nevertheless, she could swirl within her dark nature to invoke harsh punishment upon any of her Priestesses who misbehaved even slightly from the stringent rules imposed by the male priesthood of the time. A moral offence in ancient cultures carried not only the punishment of the accused by the ruling hierarchy, but also the wrath of the Goddesses in their dark aspects.

Berchta

Moving on to one more interesting deity is the less recognized Germanic deity of ancient folklore by the name of Berchta who was known as an Alpine Goddess of the Dead. She was a revered Dark Goddess in German, Swiss, and Austrian legends also known as a domestic Goddess who protected babies, children, and women by guiding their souls into the afterlife. Images of Berchta in her triple Goddess persona shows her wearing a belt with three hanging golden keys that represent birth, death, and rebirth. She has often been portrayed as a lovely maiden with long black braids that fall on either side of her head and wearing a long white gown. But her image transposes into a vision of an elderly crone in disheveled clothes. Does her story remind us of Hecate? A common misrepresentation, and not surprising is the Christian Church of the Middle Ages that rose to prominence and demonized her into becoming a child eating hag. She suddenly becomes less of a Goddess and more of a maligned woman who is evil in the eyes of the Church. Portrayed as the leader of the Wild Hunt as a spirit who along with other demons rode through the night collecting the souls of the dead.

Berchta the lovely Goddess who protected and guided babies and women was nearly stomped out with the rising power of the ancient Church. Demoted and dismissed by the new religious hierarchy, she was no longer worshipped.

A parallel fate was met by the Goddess Lilith who was also demonized as a killer of young children and babies in her persona of a night hag. Berchta starts out as a revered Goddess but like Lilith and so many others scandalized by the early Christian Church, she was turned into a sinner and never redeemed as a saint.

Endnotes

1. www.magellantv.com/articles/goddesses-of-the-ancient-world-legends-of-powerful-religious-deities
2. https://symbolsage.com/fire-goddesses-names/
3. http://www.thewhitegoddess.co.uk/divinity_of_the_day/egyptian/neith.asp

Chapter 5

Ode to the Fallen Women of Mythology

Liturgy

I am your daughter, sister, mother, and grandmother
I am a fearless Queen and Temple Priestess
I am the whore of Babylon and a saintly Goddess
I am a wife and the mother of your children
I am no sinner but hardly a saint
My memory is your mirror
I do not shun adversity
I embrace darkness and light
I have wisdom and determination
I am free-thinking and sexual
I have learned to overcome misfortune
My memory is your mirror
I understand the ancient struggles
I do not lurk in the shadows
I am proud and not humble
I fear not the apple
I do not apologize for I know who I am
My memory is your mirror
I will not fade nor hide
I embrace the Goddess but not false idols
I am fallen in your eyes but I am still here
I will always be your conscience
As I stand at the crossroads of every woman's life

Addendum to the Liturgy

Ancient text does not do me justice
For I am lost between the lines
Of scorn and desire

To be declared evil
Yet passionate and pleasing
Do I worry you?
What a contradiction of values
I've witnessed again and again
Through the millennium and beyond
Until today!

In Memoriam

Women most soiled
I mourn your fall
Sinners and Saints
Goddesses all
Rise up with praise
For your souls are avenged
Your spirits awakened
Your memories celebrated

Sinner and Saint

I am a sinner and a saint
Who lives in the light
And does not shy away from the dark
Who welcomes all the worlds desires
And shows her nakedness without fear
Propelled by the tides and the wind
I refuse to suffocate within righteousness
And for that I am deemed evil
Yet I am no fool
For my heart is pure
And my flaws mistook
Ah! the world does not accept me
And I do not agree with it!

Sinner I

Do not crush my halo
For I am your mirror
Sinner in your eyes
Saint in mine

Sinner II

Cast your stones upon my person
And see your image in my eyes
Judges, you have ignored my truth
And disregarded my humility
For I do not see my transgression
Is there no mercy for my blood?

Sinner III

Who can tame the tart
Or harness the vixen
Or reject the enchantress
Not the writer
Nor the artist
Bring on the vamps, sirens, and harlots
So lovely to see you all!

Sinner IV

I am not indifferent
I simply do not submit
I relish my strength
I stand up to falsehoods
I cannot be written away
I am here
I will stay

Hymn to the Goddess I

You are wise above all
You are grace itself
Like a dancer about to take flight
You beckon to me within my heart and soul
You are poised in the silence of the ages
And I am rooted on this earth
Far off between all time
Across the seas and through the cosmos
Blessed Matron, Blessed Healer, Goddess of the darkness and light
Your spirit calls to me
With a whisper that is your song

Hymn to the Goddess II

Dry my tears
For I am not sad
I live on in your heart
For I am the spirit of life
And the Goddess within

Hymn to the Goddess III

I do not rule the world
For I am the world
Behold my Divine power
For I am the naked brightness of the universe

Epilogue

Awareness is the essence of being. Throughout the millennium between wars, famines, natural disasters, religious and political upheavals *The Fallen Women of Mythology: Goddesses, Saints and Sinners,* our ancient heroines should never be forgotten. In fact, they are about to triumph, for in our new understanding of their collective stories they become an inspiration and revelation. Countless ancient fallen women recognized their hidden potentials within their devotion and reverence to the Goddess in her many guises, as many more are today.

Offerings are still made to the Nicaraguan Goddess, Masaya, who was thought to be an oracle. Pilgrims still pray to her for guidance and information about forthcoming volcanic disruptions and earthquakes. Another similar divinity is the Hawaiian Goddess, Pele, where even today she is revered as much as she is feared and offerings are still made to her for protection.

Witches, Pagans and Wiccans continue to boldly celebrate the seasons with ancient rituals that honor the deities of old. We should never underestimate the power that rises from women who have been misaligned or ignored, but who gained immeasurable strength by venerating the Goddess.

References

Sophia Goddess of Wisdom Bride of God, Caitlin Mathews, Quest Books

https://sophianicmth.org Sophianic Myth I The Fallen Goddess Scenario

Gaskill, Malcolm, Hellish Nell: The Last of Britain's Witches, Fourth Estate, 2001

All the Women of the Bible, M.L. Mastro, Castle Books, 2004

Tau Malachi, St. Mary Magdalene, The Gnostic Tradition of the Holy Bride, Llewellyn Publications, 2008

https://thehindutvatimes.wordpress.com//2017/05/08/petra-an-ancient-shiva-temple/

https://www.lexico.com/en/definition/fallen_woman

https://www.vagabomb.com//Defying-Countless-Prejudices-These-Women-throughout-History-Slayed-Misogynistic-Myths/

https://www.britannica.com/biography/Hatshepsut

https://medium.com/lessons-from-history/woman-was-considered-a-sinner-in-ancient-china-c9a416e5ff2d

https://otherworldlyoracle.com/ winter-gods-goddesses

https://gnosticismexplained.org/sophia/

https://www.thoughtco.com/queen-olympias-biography-3528390

https://sabbatsandsabbaths.com/2022/01/25/brigid-the-goddess-behind-the-saint/

https://www.beliefnet.com/faiths/catholic/saints/worst-sinners-who-became-saints.aspx

https://www.biblicalarchaeology.org/daily/people-cultures-in-the-bible/people-in-the-bible/scandalous-women-in-the-bible/

https://sabbatsandsabbaths.com/2022/01/25/brigid-the-goddess-behind-the-saint/

https://www.franciscanmedia.org/saint-of-the-day/saint-angela-of-foligno/

https://ca.thegospelcoalition.org/columns/ad-fontes/who-is-the-whore-of-babylon-and-why-does-it-matter/

https://www.the-bible-antichrist.com//babylon-the-great.html

https://www.biblestudytools.com/dictionary/prostitution/

https://www.gotquestions.org/life-Rahab.html

https://www.gotquestions.org/Oholah-and-Oholibah.html

https://www.thoughtco.com/artemisia-warrior-queen-of-halicarnassus-3528382

https://otherworldlyoracle.com/berchta-goddess-women-children-perchten/

https://ascensionglossary.com//index.php/Achamoth#

https://mythnerd.com//most-evil-dangerous-greek-gods-and-goddesses/#

teaandrosemary.com/dark-goddesses/

https://www.goddess-guide.com/hindu-goddess-kali.html#

You may also like

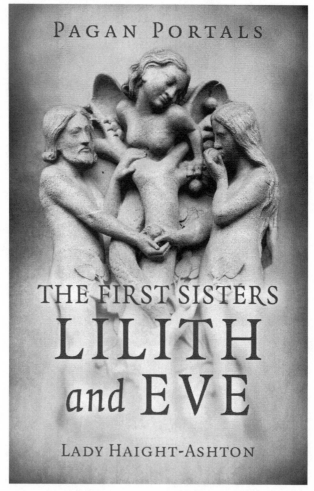

PAGAN PORTALS

THE FIRST SISTERS
LILITH
and EVE

LADY HAIGHT-ASHTON

The First Sisters: Lilith and Eve
Lady Haight-Ashton

*The tale of the first female, so troublesome she was
erased from mythology to be replaced by her sister, Eve*

978-1-78904-079-1 (Paperback)
978-1-78904-080-7 (e-book)

MOON BOOKS
PAGANISM & SHAMANISM

What is Paganism? A religion, a spirituality, an alternative belief system, nature worship? You can find support for all these definitions (and many more) in dictionaries, encyclopaedias, and text books of religion, but subscribe to any one and the truth will evade you. Above all Paganism is a creative pursuit, an encounter with reality, an exploration of meaning and an expression of the soul. Druids, Heathens, Wiccans and others, all contribute their insights and literary riches to the Pagan tradition. Moon Books invites you to begin or to deepen your own encounter, right here, right now.

If you have enjoyed this book, why not tell other readers by posting a review on your preferred book site.

Bestsellers from Moon Books

Keeping Her Keys
An Introduction to Hekate's Modern Witchcraft
Cyndi Brannen
*Blending Hekate, witchcraft and personal development
together to create a powerful new magickal perspective.*
Paperback: 978-1-78904-075-3 ebook 978-1-78904-076-0

Journey to the Dark Goddess
How to Return to Your Soul
Jane Meredith
*Discover the powerful secrets of the Dark Goddess and
transform your depression, grief and pain into healing
and integration.*
Paperback: 978-1-84694-677-6 ebook: 978-1-78099-223-5

Shamanic Reiki
Expanded Ways of Working with Universal Life Force Energy
Llyn Roberts, Robert Levy
*Shamanism and Reiki are each powerful ways of healing; together,
their power multiplies. Shamanic Reiki introduces techniques to
help healers and Reiki practitioners tap ancient healing wisdom.*
Paperback: 978-1-84694-037-8 ebook: 978-1-84694-650-9

Southern Cunning
Folkloric Witchcraft in the American South
Aaron Oberon
*Modern witchcraft with a Southern flair, this book is a
journey through the folklore of the American South and
a look at the power these stories hold for modern witches.*
Paperback: 978-1-78904-196-5 ebook: 978-1-78904-197-2

Readers of ebooks can buy or view any of these bestsellers by clicking on the live link in the title. Most titles are published in paperback and as an ebook. Paperbacks are available in traditional bookshops. Both print and ebook formats are available online.

Find more titles and sign up to our readers' newsletter www.collectiveinkbooks.com/paganism

For video content, author interviews and more, please subscribe to our YouTube channel.

MoonBooksPublishing

Follow us on social media for book news, promotions and more:

Facebook: Moon Books

Instagram: @MoonBooksCI

X: @MoonBooksCI

TikTok: @MoonBooksCI